Test the Nation

Test the Nation
The IQ Book

by Colin Cooper

BBC

To Brian and Joan Jepson
With whom I imagined I was talking

This book is published to accompany the programme
Test the Nation – The National IQ Test, based on a format
devised by Eyeworks TV and produced by Talent TV.
First broadcast in the UK in May 2002. *Test the Nation –
The National IQ Test* 2002 © Eyeworks/RTL/Talent

Executive Producers: John Kaye Cooper and Reinout Oerlemans
Producer: Nicholas Hegarty
Content Producer: Jean Davison
Director: Simon Staffurth

Published by BBC Worldwide Limited, Woodlands,
80 Wood Lane, London W12 0TT
First published 2003

ISBN 0 563 48745 3

Commissioning Editor: Emma Shackleton
Project Editor: Julia Charles
Copy Editor: Tessa Clark
Designer: DW Design, London
Production Controller: Kenneth MacKay

Set in Minion and Reaction Ultra
Printed and bound in Great Britain by Mackays of Chatham Ltd
Cover printed by Belmont Press Ltd, Northampton.

Introduction

Intelligence tests are everywhere. Job applicants worldwide are likely to be given a psychological test to determine how suited they are for a particular post. Our children may be given ability tests if they seem to have problems at school, or as part of a career-counselling process. When the elderly are admitted to hospital a simple test is often used to alert physicians to the possibility of dementia. In countries such as the United States, intelligence tests are used to determine which university children should attend. And most remarkably of all, people even choose to spend their spare time taking IQ tests presented via television and the Internet!

So what are these tests? How are they constructed? What influences how well a particular person will perform? Is it really possible or sensible to describe all of a person's myriad abilities using one number, their IQ? How can performance on these tests be improved? Are the tests fair? And most crucially, does how well a person performs on these simple tests predict anything else useful about their behaviour?

This book attempts to address as many of these issues as possible, with emphasis on the interesting and practical issues. For example, are differences in IQ related to how long people are likely to live? What can you do to prepare yourself for an ability test at work? Are there any 'tricks' that you can learn which might allow you to perform better than the next person?

Does giving young children a lot of stimulation make them into smart adults? What *causes* people to vary in their IQs? The book is aimed squarely at the nonspecialist – for example, the person who has recently taken an intelligence test and is curious about what their IQ implies, or who is sceptical as to whether it is possible to assess human intelligence.

The idea for the book came about following the *National IQ Test* – a television programme that has allowed viewers in many countries to assess their IQ (Intelligence Quotient) via television. I became involved when Jean Davison, a producer at Talent TV, needed to develop a test for the British version of the programme. It was a challenging proposition, but thanks to Jean's expert tutelage and enthusiasm the test was developed and standardized in record time. I was frankly amazed by the amount of interest it generated. Suddenly IQ-testing was transformed from an academic discipline into a topic of conversation around the world's water-coolers, and a flood of e-mails, newsgroup threads and discussion group entries showed that we all want to find out more about how IQ is defined, what a particular IQ implies, whether/how IQ can be boosted, how it changes over a person's life span and so on.

Popular psychology books are sometimes written to promote a particular idea or a novel theory, whereas this one tries to give a balanced view of IQ that is informed by the scientific literature – that is, by hard data derived from experiments, rather than by speculation. But rest assured that this is not a textbook; most of the issues that interest psychologists these days are dealt with in a single chapter (Chapter 8) and I have assumed no knowledge of psychology or statistics.

I have included the UK version of the National IQ Test in the book, along with instructions for scoring it and converting the score into an IQ. So, providing there is no cheating (for example, by taking a look at the questions beforehand!) it should be possible for readers to take the test and estimate their IQ. Unless you have already taken it, you will probably want to do so before reading the book as what is discussed in the text will seem a lot more concrete and real once you have had the experience of taking the test. And the earlier you take it, the less likely it is that you will sneak a look at the items beforehand!

The first two chapters give some background information about what is meant by 'abilities', how ability tests are constructed and why it is legitimate to average the scores obtained from different types of problems in order to estimate a person's general intelligence. Chapter 3 looks at what is meant by Intelligence Quotient, how scores from tests are translated into IQs and how IQ scores should be interpreted. Chapters 4, 5 and 6 look at whether IQ typically changes much over a person's life span, whether scores on tests can be boosted through practice or training, and offer some practical tips for increasing test performance. Chapter 7 discusses whether scores on IQ tests can predict anything about how people behave in the real world, and Chapter 8 introduces the sorts of questions that are now being researched in universities worldwide. Finally, Chapter 9 addresses some 'frequently asked questions' about IQ that emerged following the *National IQ Test* broadcast.

It still strikes me as amazing that people perform at similar levels when solving very different types of problem – for example, those who are fortunate enough to have excellent memories will also tend to be able to visualize things well, come up with creative ideas and indeed perform above average on virtually *all* tasks that require thought. Logically it need not be so. For example, it is not the case that all of these skills require language or logical 'convergent' reasoning. Very few, if any, findings in psychology are as general as this, as obvious or as frequently replicated.

A person's IQ is, arguably, one of their most important characteristics; you can probably predict their behaviour better from their IQ than from any other single piece of information about them. It is also an area of psychology rife with myth, prejudice and misunderstanding. If, as a reader of this book , you come away with a clearer idea of what IQ is, how it is assessed, what it can predict and some of its causes, then I shall be well satisfied.

Belfast
December, 2002

Chapter 1

Intelligence, mental abilities and tests

Over the years plenty of attempts have been made to define the term 'intelligence'. For example, in 1923 the American psychologist Edwin G. Boring[1] asked a number of other eminent psychologists to explain what they meant by the term and received a huge range of definitions as each of them thought that the aspect of intelligence he or she was studying was the most important. Most mentioned that intelligence involved thought or reasoning – for example, the capacity to reason logically, to solve problems, to think in abstract terms or to process information quickly. Other definitions were less helpful – for example, 'intelligence is that which intelligence tests measure' (which begs the problem that different tests might perhaps measure quite different things). But, by and large, the answers suggested that each person has a particular level of 'intelligence' that will influence how well (and perhaps also how fast) they will perform a range of tasks that require thought for their successful completion. However, this simple definition involves making two huge assumptions.

The first is that there is, indeed, only one type of intelligence and this influences performance on *all* tasks requiring thought. Some critics have argued that this is quite wrong, and we should look at a whole range of different skills – for example, we should consider a person's skill with language, their memory, their ability to deal with numbers, how well they can visualize things

– and perhaps even their skill at getting on with other people. So, rather than speaking of 'intelligence', we should perhaps draw up a profile of abilities for each person, as it is likely that each individual will excel in some areas whilst performing less well in others. Chapter 2 examines which of these two views is best supported by the facts.

The second assumption is that intelligence actually exists. It is very easy to fall into the trap of labelling something and deluding ourselves that, because we have done so, we somehow have a proper scientific grasp of what it is all about. Just because we observe that some people perform better when solving puzzles than others, it is tempting to say that the reason why they perform better is because they are more intelligent. But that simply does not follow. It is like saying that water is wet because wetness is a property of water; how could it be otherwise? It is simply a way of summarizing what has been observed. A scientific explanation must go beyond describing the facts: it should attempt to explain them in terms of simpler things. So a scientific theory of intelligence should explain what *causes* people to vary in their problem-solving ability – perhaps in terms of their upbringing, the sort of schooling they received, their social background, their genetic make-up or the way their nervous system operates.

For now, however, I will talk in terms of 'mental abilities' rather than intelligence, and will not begin to speculate on how many different abilities are required to describe a person's performance. Psychologists who are interested in how people differ from each other usually classify people in four ways. Personality reflects a person's 'personal style' – their way of doing things. For example, some people may be cheerful and optimistic in just about every situation, whilst others may exude a fog of gloom and despondency. Several of these personality traits have been identified and researched in detail, but this book is not the place to explore such work. Those studying moods and emotions are interested in short-term feelings. For example, it has been found that apparently trivial events such as finding a coin put us into a good mood, and that we all tend to feel jaded on Mondays. Psychologists studying motivation try to understand why people do things. What drives some people to spend their free time helping others, travelling or collecting antiques? Finally, the psychology of mental abilities investigates how well people can solve problems that require thought, and what makes some people better than others at doing so.

Mental abilities and conscious thought

This book focuses on mental abilities, as reflected in tasks (a) that require thought and (b) where the quality of the solution can be assessed. Solving a crossword, deciding on the fastest route through the supermarket, deciphering the instructions for self-assembly furniture and diagnosing what is wrong with an ailing car or computer are all examples of everyday tasks that involve thought, and where the quality of the solution may be evaluated. For example, we could count the number of clues correctly answered, time the supermarket run, note the number of mistakes made when assembling the furniture or the time it takes to do so, and ask a panel of judges to rate how good the fault-diagnosis was. However, with all these tasks, how well a person performs is likely to reflect experience and motivation as well as raw reasoning ability. The person who has been doing crosswords for 20 years, or who feels they need to complete them to boost their self-esteem, is likely to perform better than someone who idly picks up a newspaper and tries a crossword for the first time. Previous experience with self-assembly furniture, faulty engines, misbehaving computers and supermarket runs will lead to good performance as a result of memory, not just reasoning.

The definition of intelligence should be widened to say that mental abilities are revealed via performance on tasks that require *conscious* thought. This is necessary since the human visual system (for example) routinely performs wonders of recognizing objects and re-creating a three-dimensional view of the world without our ever being aware of it, and we do not want our definition of intelligence to consider variations in these sorts of skills.

The key thing about these mental abilities is that they supposedly measure a person's ability to apply thought in a huge variety of settings. They are therefore quite unlike tests of knowledge or attainment – for example, where children are asked to learn a page of French irregular verbs, remember which characteristics define a living organism or recite the state capitals of the United States. The results of such tests are not good measures of mental abilities for two reasons. First, the child's performance is likely to be heavily influenced by his or her motivation to learn the material: a highly able child who looks at the material for the first time on the train on the way to school may get the same score as a less able one who spent hours on their homework. Second, the tests of French grammar and biological and geographical knowledge simply assess how well the child has absorbed what has been taught. The fact that a child knows all the state capitals in the USA, for example, does not guarantee that they will know anything at all about the physical geography of Australasia or any other geographical topic: they may not have been asked to learn these facts. These assessments have been designed to measure how well a child can soak up specific knowledge, not how well they can think and reason.

This is actually something of a simplification. Assessments of how well a person can comprehend a passage of text or simplify arithmetic expressions probably measure intelligence as much as knowledge. But whilst high intelligence may make it easier for some people to memorize and retain information, a prodigious knowledge of trivial facts (for example) does not imply a high mental ability. Mental abilities involve thought and applying knowledge to new situations.

Measuring the mind

Psychologists have three main ways of assessing people's behaviour. The first involves trained raters observing how people act in a wide range of settings, and rating them on certain characteristics. This has been used in personality research, where raters notice whether (for example) the person initiates conversations with strangers, responds positively to requests for help, speeds up when walking through a lonely place at night and so on. However, such research is expensive (raters have to be trained and paid, and each must observe a single individual for long periods of time) and so it is not commonly used. There is also the problem that the presence of the rater may influence behaviour: a lonely street is not quite so lonely when one is followed around by someone with a clipboard! It would be possible to estimate various abilities by this method (for example, noting whether a person takes the shortest route, remembers what they need at the shops, is able to tender the correct money) but because of the expense this technique is rarely used. Another difficulty with this approach is that we all encounter different problems in our everyday life. Is someone who can think up a novel way of unblocking a sink more or less intelligent than the research scientist who fails to make an important connection between two pieces of evidence? Because the problems differ so much in difficulty, it is impossible to tell. However, teachers' ratings may be useful estimates of a child's abilities, although other factors (such as whether the teacher likes the child and how willing the child is to answer questions in class) can, and do, distort the ratings.

The second possibility is to use self-report questionnaires. These are widely used to assess personality. Here people are given questionnaires which ask them to rate how well phrases such as 'I sometimes feel nervous when in crowds' or 'I do not worry too much about making mistakes' describe them. There are some obvious and well-researched problems with this sort of technique. Where does the person decide to draw the line between 'feeling nervous' and 'not feeling nervous' – will different people use different criteria? And will people tend to portray themselves in a favourable light? This technique could be used to assess abilities by using items such as 'I am better than most people at solving problems that require careful, logical thought' or 'My memory often lets me down' – but the problem is that people are unlikely to *know* how their mental skills compare with those of the general population. So, whilst people would probably be quite willing to answer an item like the one below, it does not follow that their answers will be accurate.

How intelligent are you:
  (a) Very intelligent
  (b) Fairly intelligent
  (c) Average
  (d) Somewhat below the average
  (e) Well below average

Although this approach has been used occasionally it is probably best avoided.

The third technique involves the measurement of behaviour in standard settings. This can involve measuring electrical activity of the brain or muscles, or observing how a person reacts to a particular event – for example, when they are faced with someone who has apparently fainted. By using the same problems for all people, the main difficulty of the ratings method (that everyone meets different challenges in their day-to-day lives) is overcome. Almost all attempts to measure mental abilities therefore use tests in which the person is asked to *demonstrate* their level of intelligence by solving a standard set of novel problems. For example, they may be asked to find a symbol that completes a series or to solve an anagram, such as 'oat top' (if that one is too easy, try 'an IBM user').

The problems should vary in difficulty because of the amount of thought required to solve them, not because of the knowledge needed to understand them. For example, 'Skywalker is to Vader as XXX is to...' would be impossible for someone who did not watch films, yet might well measure intelligence amongst those who do. The context of the problems should be unfamiliar, so that everyone taking the test has to reason out the correct solution rather than rely on knowledge. For example, suppose people were to solve the following problem. 'A metalworking factory uses a drill to bore out holes in metal, but sharp fragments of metal fall off the drill and into the hole, and this causes problems further down the production line. What is the simplest solution you can think of?' Most people would have to think through a list of possible answers – for example, blasts of air, magnets (probably not a good idea as they're not told what sort of metal is being drilled) and performing the drilling upside down so that the debris would just fall out. But an engineer, or someone who works in this type of factory, would probably have come across the problem before and would be able to come up with an instant solution. So the reason why most items in ability tests seem rather abstract is to ensure that no one will have encountered anything like them before.

Ability tests

Ability tests are simply sets of problems that depend on thought for their successful completion and whose context is likely to be familiar to everyone (or to no one). As an example of a familiar context, we might ask what the next letter would be in the sequence b, c, d, f, g, h – since we could probably assume that everyone answering the question knows about vowels and consonants. But if we asked people to complete the sequence a, s, d, f, g, those who were not familiar with the layout of UK keyboards could not possibly answer it correctly (they are the letters at the start of the middle row of the standard typewriter/computer keyboard). An example of a problem with which no one would be familiar would be to ask people to visualize what a particular shape would look like if it were rotated or to memorize a tune that they had not heard before.

The type of response required from the person being assessed will vary from test to test. Some tests will ask him or her to select one answer from several (usually about four) possible alternatives – a multiple-choice test. Test-constructors are often cunning when thinking up plausible alternatives, trying to anticipate responses that would result from using some common (but incorrect) strategy. For example, if someone setting a test were to ask a person to estimate roughly what 93 divided by 2.5 was, they would probably include 37 (the correct answer), 3.7 (in case someone got confused with the decimal point), 0.027 (2.5 divided by 93), etc. Such items are invariably tried out before use in order to check that the wrong answers are equally often chosen by people who are forced to guess. Other tests may ask the person to write down the correct answer, which is then scored. Such items can be problematical: for example, if a child were asked to define 'kitten' and wrote 'a sort of cat' it is not quite clear whether they have grasped the precise meaning of the word.

There are few hard and fast rules about how the items should be presented. Some tests have time limits: others may give people as long as they want to solve the items. Some tests consist of many items that are very similar to each other in content (which can become a little tedious for the person taking the test). Others mix several types of item on the same page: a mental arithmetic puzzle may be followed by an anagram which is followed by a maze, for example. Other tests may have separate timed sections: 20 mazes, 20 arithmetic puzzles, etc. whilst computerized and televised tests may allow a specific amount of time for each item. The time limits are usually established by administering the test (or item, or section) without time limits to a sample of people whilst the test is being constructed, and noting how long it usually takes them to complete it. This information is then used to set appropriate time limits for the test.

It is usual to place the easy items towards the start of each test (or section) and the harder items towards the end, so that people's confidence will be boosted when they get the first few items correct and they will not waste time struggling with a very difficult item that is presented early. The difficulty of each item is established whilst the test is being constructed by administering the items to a sample of people and noting the proportion who get each item wrong.

Ability tests are simply collections of such items which are given to people in a standard way, so that it should not matter who administers the test – the instructions given, the practice items that are shown beforehand, the time taken to solve the items, the type of response required and even the layout of the answer sheet are all carefully controlled. Test-takers should be told whether or not to guess if they are uncertain of the correct answer, as some tests penalize wrong guesses whilst most do not. The test items should be in large print so that those with less-than-perfect vision are not disadvantaged, and there are detailed instructions for administering each test – even standard answers that should be given if anyone asks a question about what they are supposed to do. The main aim is to ensure that performance on the test items reflects the ability that is being assessed, with the influence of other factors (test anxiety, motivation, mood, distractions, etc.) minimized as far as possible by the warm social skills of the person administering the test, and the sensitive choice of testing conditions.

Types of test

Ability tests are now commonly given via computers, as this

makes life easier for the test-administrators – it is easy for the computer to ensure that items are presented for precise time limits and the scoring of responses is both automatic and accurate. However, there are examples of some truly horrible computerized tests that are still on the market. One, for example, asks people to choose the correct answer by pressing the a, b, c or d key on the keyboard. Points are awarded for speed, so skilled keyboard-users will have an unfair advantage over those of us who are two-fingered typists and have to search for every letter. Some tests ('adaptive tests' or 'tailored tests') are based on sophisticated statistical theory which allows each candidate to be given a different set of test items, so that they are not bored by seeing items that they find very easy or daunted by too many difficult ones. What is clever about these tests is that although people have been given quite different items it is possible to compare their abilities. If everyone has taken the same items people can be compared by simply counting the number of items that have been answered correctly. This cannot be done with tailored tests, as one person may have been given 50 easy items whilst someone else may have been given 50 difficult ones: if both get 30 out of 50 correct this does not imply that they have the same ability. But the huge majority of tests in current use simply count up the number of items that have been answered correctly, and interpret this as a measure of how well a person performed.

Some tests are designed for groups of people, whereas others require one-to-one interaction between a trained psychologist and the person being assessed. Group tests are often given when screening people as part of the selection process for a job, and (sometimes) to determine whether a pupil should attend an academically demanding school or a top-ranking university or college. Tests involving one-to-one interaction are expensive to administer and so are usually used only when particularly precise assessments are required – for example, when assessing whether a child has special educational needs or problems using language (dyslexia), or to discover whether someone who has been accused of a crime is intelligent enough to be able to understand that what they did was wrong.

Tests should be as long as possible as it can be shown that the accuracy of the score improves the more items there are. For example, in a two-item test where each item has four possible alternatives, the chances of someone with very low ability correctly guessing all the items (and so scoring 2 though their 'true' ability is zero will be $\frac{1}{4} \times \frac{1}{4} = \frac{1}{16}$). With a ten-item test the chance of the person getting 10 out of 10 through random guessing is so small as to be negligible. Long tests also make it possible to include a wider range of items, to ensure that no one is 'lucky' or 'unlucky' by being presented with ones they find unusually easy or difficult – for example, because they have seen a particular problem before or it relates to some specific skill they may have. When assessing cooking knowledge via the item 'When making batter, which is the first ingredient normally added to the flour?' it is possible that amongst the people taking the test there will be someone whose only cooking knowledge lies in making pancakes (and whose correct answer will cause their skill to be overestimated) whilst an accomplished cook may suffer a mental block and choose 'milk' rather than 'egg'. If a test consists of a large number of items these lucky (or unlucky) accidents will have less impact on the total score. However, if a test is too long those taking it will become tired, bored or lose concentration. So it is rare for an individual test to last much longer than 40 or 50 minutes.

Scoring tests

We now know that an ability test consists of several items, each of which has a clearly defined, single correct response. It is usual to give one point for a 'correct' answer and zero points for an 'incorrect' one; some tests will even subtract a point for a wrong answer if the instructions say clearly that those taking the test should not guess if they are unsure. Items that are not attempted are usually treated as if they were answered incorrectly and receive zero points.

The end result when someone has taken a test and the items have been scored is a string of 1s and 0s, one per item. The really thorny issue is knowing what to do with all this information. It is clear that adding together items that measure different things is meaningless, in just the same way that it would be meaningless to describe a journey by adding together the distance travelled in kilometres and the time taken in minutes. A 60-minute, 600-kilometre journey by aeroplane would give the same result (660) as a 10-hour hike over 60 kilometres, so if you told someone you had undertaken a '660 unit journey' this would not convey any useful information.

Exactly the same principle applies when using psychological tests. For example, suppose that people were given the following four-item personality questionnaire:

(a) I always check my bank statements carefully for errors.
(b) When I am out of my home I sometimes worry that I have left lights or appliances switched on.
(c) I'm at my best when I'm with a large group of friends.
(d) A good party is the best way to celebrate.

Here the first two items measure 'obsessionality', or attention to detail, and the second two measure sociability. Suppose that answering 'Yes' to a question gains you one point and answering 'No' gets zero points. What would you make of someone's personality if they told you that they scored two points on this test? It would not be possible to draw any sensible inference at all: the person might be obsessional but unsocial (scoring 1, 1, 0, 0), 'laid back' and sociable (0, 0, 1, 1) or mildly obsessional and mildly sociable (1, 0, 0, 1; 0, 1, 0, 1; 1, 0, 1, 0 or 0, 1, 1, 0). So it only makes sense to add scores on items together if these items measure the same thing.

It may sometimes be possible to decide beforehand which items together measure a single characteristic. For example, clinical psychologists and psychiatrists know rather a lot about conditions such as depression. As well as reporting sad, depressed mood a seriously depressed person will show changes in behaviour (for example, becoming lethargic, waking early in the morning), disturbances of thought (for example, feeling that there is no hope that the condition will ever improve) and so on. Since these are all clinical indicators of depression the first step in constructing a questionnaire measuring depression would be to write some items that may assess these behaviours and feelings, and score this questionnaire by assigning one point for each one that is answered in the 'depressed' direction.

However, it is not always possible to do this. For example, suppose that the aim was to assess a group of school-leavers' prowess at mathematics. We could put together some problems that assess addition, subtraction, division, multiplication, algebra, geometry, matrices, etc. But are these all measures of a single mathematical ability? Or might it be the case that some children excel at tasks requiring visualization, and so will perform well at geometry; in other words, for them might geometry be quite different from the other tasks? It is not particularly scientific to try to resolve this issue by speculating about what one *thinks* should happen – what if several different researchers think different things? How can we tell who (if anyone) is correct? One of the characteristics that distinguishes psychology from philosophy is its reliance on real-life data. Faced with the sort of problem outlined above, a psychologist's first reaction will be to go out and *measure* how school-leavers actually perform on a wide range of mathematical test items, and then use statistical techniques to determine how many different types of mathematical skills there are.

To further complicate matters, it is not possible to construct a test simply by writing down a few items 'off the top of one's head' and assume that they measure what you intend them to measure. For example, consider the following item for a mathematics test:

> The perimeter of a rectangular sports pitch is always at least twice its length: true or false.

Someone who did not know the meaning of the word 'perimeter' would not be able to solve the item and so would only have a 50-50 chance of guessing the correct answer, whereas for someone does know the meaning of 'perimeter' the item is trivially easy. This 'mathematical' item could well measure vocabulary! So the test-construction process involves writing items, administering them to a large sample of people and then analysing precisely what they assess.

Factor analysis

A statistical tool called 'factor analysis' has been developed to determine how many distinct abilities are measured by a set of ability items. It involves giving ability items to a sample of several hundred people. Each person's response to each question is then scored as correct or incorrect, and these numbers are fed into a computer package. The results of the analysis will show (a) how many distinct abilities are measured by the items, and (b) which items measure each of these abilities. It therefore shows us how the test should be scored. For example, consider the four-item personality questionnaire on page 23. If this was given to 100 people and the results were factor analysed, then the computer output would almost certainly show that the four items measured two distinct personality characteristics. Factor analysis would show that the first two items measured one characteristic, whilst the third and fourth items measured a completely different aspect of personality. So in order to draw any inferences about personality from this test it would be necessary to calculate two different scores for each person who took the test, one based on the first two items and the other based on the last two. Given the nature of the questions, this is hardly surprising! But the key point is that it is not necessary to 'tell' the computer program how many different abilities (or personality characteristics) are measured by a set of items, or which item(s) you think measure which ability. Instead we just give a large number of items to a large sample of people, score the responses, perform a factor analysis and see how many different factors emerge. We then name the factors by looking at the content of the items. For example, as the first two items on page 23 ask about attention to detail we might tentatively label the factor formed by these two items 'carefulness', 'obsessionality' or something similar. If there is such a thing as 'intelligence', factor analysis will show that each of the items in a test measures a single dimension ('factor') of ability.

Factor analysis can offer a way of deciding how to combine the scores of test items meaningfully in order to describe a person's mental abilities. How many different dimensions ('factors') are necessary to do so? Can we add together the scores from all the items in the test and speak of a factor of 'general intelligence', or should we derive one score for the verbal items, another score based on the items that require visualization, another score for the memory items and so on – so that we summarize a person's mental abilities using perhaps ten different terms? Psychologists have studied this problem for almost a century and there is now general agreement about the structure of human abilities, as discussed in the next chapter. This is important as it tells us whether it is possible to summarize a person's abilities using one term (for example, 'general intelligence') or whether it is necessary to draw up a profile of abilities for each person, showing (for example) that one individual has excellent memory, average numerical skills and below-average verbal and visualization skills, whilst someone else has a quite different profile. The important thing to remember is that the models of ability discussed in the next chapter are based on hard facts, not intuition or theoretical speculation.

Summary

This chapter has defined the term 'mental ability' and tried to show how psychologists have gone about measuring mental abilities using tests. It outlined why it only makes sense to add up scores on several items if they measure the same thing, and shows that factor analysis can be used to find out how many different mental abilities are measured by any particular collection of test items. The results of such analyses are described in Chapter 2.

Chapter 2

The discovery of General Intelligence

Towards the end of the nineteenth century the Victorians were keen to apply the techniques of physics to human functioning. Several experimenters (for example, the scientist Sir Francis Galton in Britain and the German-born anthropologist Franz Boas in the United States) assessed people for hearing, eyesight, head size, ability to remember the duration of a sound, ability to distinguish small differences in pitch or loudness, the speed with which a person could respond to a sound and so on, and attempted to discover whether any of these could predict how well a person performed in school or in society.

It is not always obvious why these particular tasks were chosen; many appear to have been borrowed from other areas of research which focused on how people in general behave. An example is work then undertaken in Germany which showed that it was the percentage increase in the strength of a stimulus that was detectable: not its absolute value. If someone was given two weights to hold they might just be able to distinguish a weight of 105 grams as being heavier than one of 100 grams. Surprisingly, they would be unable to tell whether a 405 gram weight was heavier or lighter than a 400 gram weight. Instead the percentage difference is all-important. One individual may be able to detect a 5% difference between two weights so would just be able to recognize that a 420 gram weight was heavier than a 400 gram one, or that a 1050 gram weight was heavier than a 1000 gram one. Many of these earlier studies therefore simply looked at the size in the variations from person to person in the tasks. Nothing of great interest was found, probably because the tests did not rely much on reasoning, and were usually performed on very small samples of people.

Other researchers focused more on thinking. For example, in the late 19th century the German experimental psychologists Hermann Ebinghaus and Axel Oehrn studied the link between memory, the ability to add up and school performance. But the French psychologist Alfred Binet thought it was self-evident that people varied along a single dimension of intelligence, and developed the first intelligence test in 1895 in order to identify children who had special educational needs. His test measured 'Memory, Mental Images, Imagination, Attention, Faculty of Comprehending, Suggestibility, Aesthetic Sentiment, Moral Sentiments, Muscular Force and Force of Will, Cleverness and "Coup d'oeil"', this last being susceptibility to illusions. Scores on these tests were added up to produce an overall estimate of intelligence. Binet and his students had no evidence that there was a single dimension of intelligence, they just assumed that it was the obvious way to categorize people.

Charles Spearman, a retired army officer, cousin of Charles Darwin and amateur scientist was quite dismissive of this work. In an article published in the *American Journal of Psychology* in 1904 he wrote: 'Hitherto, these had been of the most elementary and unequivocal nature possible, as befits the rigor of scientific work... Binet and Henri appear now to... [be] sacrificing much of the elementariness... The result would seem likely to have more practical than theoretical value.'[1] However, Binet's work inspired Spearman to address the fundamental question of the relationship between the scores on all of the tests. Do they assess quite different mental abilities? Or is it the case that people who perform well on one test also perform well on some or all of the others?

One type of mental ability or many?

To determine whether the intuitive assumptions made by Binet, Galton and others were in fact accurate, Spearman decided to gather some data to settle the matter. He also had to invent the statistical technique needed to analyse these data. His long paper in the *American Journal of Psychology* is still regarded as a landmark publication in intelligence research.

Spearman's approach was simple. He assembled a few psychological tests which he thought might assess different aspects of thinking and reasoning, administered them to samples of schoolchildren and performed factor analysis to determine whether all the tests and test items reflected a single dimension of intelligence, or whether they measured several different mental abilities. Judged by today's standards, Spearman's work was crude. The tests he used measured ability to detect small differences in the pitch of sounds, shades of grey, and differences in weight, together with tests assessing memory. He also included examination results for mathematics, English, etc and teachers' ratings of common sense and intelligence. The study involved young children in two schools: a village school and 'a preparatory school of the highest class, which principally trained boys for Harrow', where 'a small prize was offered to stimulate attention, and energetic measures were found necessary to prevent cribbing [cheating]'. Spearman analyzed the relationships between the scores on the tests, not the relationships between individual items in the tests. For example, he *assumed* that all the arithmetic items measured a single 'numerical ability' and added together the scores on all the addition, subtraction etc. items. Then he applied factor analysis to the test scores to discover if there was one, or more than one, type of 'intelligence'.

The important result from this experiment was that children who tended to be near the top of their class in one area (for example, mathematics) also tended to produce excellent scores on all the other tests. Those who showed average performance on one test also tended to show average performance on all the others. And those who performed well below average on one test also performed poorly on all the others. This led Spearman to conclude that it was, in fact, reasonable to average scores across all the tests to produce a single score which he called 'general intelligence', also known as 'general ability' and often abbreviated to *g*. He called this *general* intelligence because it was general to all tasks: a person who had a high level of *g* would perform well in any task that required thought and reasoning for its successful completion. From Spearman's work, it seems that Binet, Galton and others were correct when they assumed that one could describe a person's repertoire of mental skills using just one number, their level of *g*, which could be estimated by averaging performance across a number of different tests.

More sophisticated methods

This finding did not remain unchallenged for long. Other researchers developed more sophisticated methods of factor analysis, tested larger samples of children and adults, and used a wider range of tests than Spearman. Unfortunately, several researchers failed to confirm Spearman's discovery that a single dimension, *g*, explains how well a child or adult will perform on just about every task. For example, in the 1930s Louis Thurstone in Chicago gave university students 56 different tests, and discovered not one dimension of ability but (eventually) about a dozen![2] He named these 'primary mental abilities' (PMAs) and developed tests to measure them. The main PMAs identified by Thurstone were:

> Verbal comprehension
> Word fluency (anagrams etc.)
> Number facility
> Spatial visualization
> Memory for associated concepts
> Perceptual speed
> Reasoning

Thus, according to Thurstone it made little sense to average performance across all tests, as Spearman had done, to obtain a measure of *g*. Instead, if to describe a person's cognitive abilities it would be necessary to report the scores on seven or more separate dimensions. There seemed to be no such thing as *g*.

The debate rumbled on, acrimoniously, in the scientific journals for years, and those who were not specialists in the area (and who were therefore unable to understand the subtleties of factor analysis) appear to have rather lost interest in the issue. This is unfortunate, as it is now known that there were several important differences between Spearman and Thurstone in the types of data and types of analyses they favoured, which made it almost inevitable that they would reach different conclusions. I outline the main issues in my 1999 book *Intelligence and Abilities*.

The modern view

There is now near-universal agreement about the true structure of mental abilities, thanks largely to the work of John B. Carroll at the University of North Carolina, who spent several years in the 1990s carefully reanalysing all known sets of data in order to map out the main abilities.[3] His work and that of others shows that both Thurstone and Spearman were correct. When responses to test items are analysed there are at least 50 narrow 'primary mental abilities', rather as Thurstone suggested. These are narrow in scope: for example, some of the primary mental abilities associated with memory include:

> Ability to memorize meaningless 'words' -- for example, womp, thrub
> Ability to memorize pairs of associated words – for example, 'old' and 'book', 'happy' and 'child'
> Memory for faces
> Ability to recall events from everyday life – for example, the colour of the carpet in your boss's office

But Thurstone was quite wrong when he thought that these narrow memory factors were completely distinct from each other. They show considerable overlap. Someone who performs well on one task also tends to perform well on the others. So it is possible to describe the structure of abilities using a diagram rather like that shown in Figure One (page 34).

This shows part of a very wide diagram. The squares at the bottom represent the individual tests. The ovals represent factors, or abilities, derived using factor analysis – the primary mental abilities (PMAs). The 'deduction' PMA would involve applying a rule – for example, if all rugby players drink beer and John is a rugby player, then by inference John will drink beer. 'Induction' involves spotting and then applying a rule, as with number series (1, 2, 4, 8...) or letter series (a, e, i, o).

A line joining a test to an oval shows that a particular test measures this particular PMA. At the next level up there are about eight 'second-order (secondary) abilities'. These are found because various PMAs are themselves quite strongly correlated. People with high scores on one of these primary mental abilities also tend to have high scores on some of the

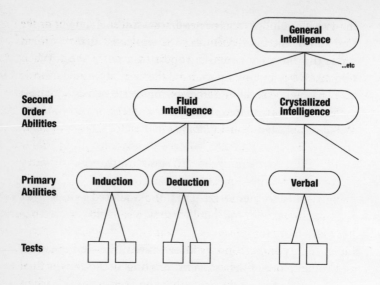

Part of a diagram showing the links between tests, primary mental abilities, second order abilities, and general intelligence

Figure One

others: hence they may be combined to form these second-order abilities. These second-order abilities all overlap considerably, so at the top of the hierarchy as a single third-order factor is Spearman's factor of general intelligence, or *g*. Therefore, when describing or assessing a person's repertoire of cognitive skills we can speak in terms of a profile of 50 or so PMAs, the eight main second-order abilities or factors, or general intelligence. An example may make this clearer.

Suppose that instead of testing people you asked them to rate (on a seven-point scale) how much they enjoyed certain films. The list of films would be a long one, and should cover the whole spectrum, just as a great many varied tasks are administered when researching the structure of abilities. It would be easy to factor-analyse people's responses to the various films using a standard statistics package. Remember that factor analysis will try to identify variables that different individuals will like to a similar extent, and so *Gunfight at the O.K. Corral* and *The Magnificent Seven* would probably form one primary factor (which might be called 'Westerns'), *Reservoir Dogs* and *Pulp Fiction* another ('urban reality' films), and *Alien* and one of the *Star Trek* films may well form a third (science fiction) factor. *When Harry Met Sally* and *Pretty Woman* might be a fourth ('romantic') factor, *Police Academy* and *The Full Monty* a fifth ('comedy') factor and *A Nightmare on Elm Street* and *Friday the 13th* a sixth ('horror') primary factor. Factor-analysing the correlations between these six primary factors might well reveal three secondary factors. I would guess that the first of these would comprise the science fiction and horror factors, and so might be labelled 'fantasy films', the second secondary factor might include 'romantic' and 'comedy' ones (perhaps called 'relaxing films') and the final secondary factor might show that the Westerns and urban reality films went together ('violent films'). Finally the correlations between these three second-order factors could be factor-analysed to obtain a single, general factor.

Now consider how you might explain why a particular person likes any particular film – *Alien*, for example. At the narrowest level of generalization (primary factor) the explanation could be that people tend to like science fiction films to a certain, characteristic extent, and this is why the individual enjoys *Alien*. Or we could move up a level, and note that the factor analysis reveals that some people enjoy fantasy films (of which science fiction is one example) whilst others do not, and *this* is why *Alien* appeals – the person may enjoy *Alien* because it is a fantasy film. Or we could explain it by resorting to the third-order factor, which reveals that some people like *all sorts* of films (of which fantasy films are one example) whilst others are not keen on any films. Our viewer might enjoy *Alien* just because he or she enjoys *all* films. But all three explanations are correct, and useful in trying to explain why an individual may enjoy the film. Which level of explanation is used ('because the person likes films', 'because they like fantasy films' or 'because they like science fiction films') is entirely up to us.[4]

Some proponents of factor analysis, notably Raymond B. Cattell, who was a prolific researcher into personality and intelligence from the 1930s to 1980s, have argued that the factors that emerge from a factor analysis offer more than just a convenient description of abilities. He argues that the factors may indicate real causal influences, and points to examples where, if some behaviours and symptoms of people with various diseases are factor-analysed, the factors that emerge correspond to various bacteria, viruses and so on. According to this 'strong' view, the factors that emerge from the analysis of human abilities may correspond to properties of the brain or nervous system, or the effects of education. For example, some people may have brain structures which have developed so as to make them particularly good at spatial problems (a second-order factor). Individual differences in general ability (g) may just indicate that some people are better than others at processing all sorts of information.

This correspondence between factors and brain function is not widely accepted, and I would not want to push the analogy too far. But imagine what one would find if one were to factor-analyse the performance of computers rather than people. Computer scientists have devised some standard benchmark tests that are designed to see how quickly a computer can perform a particular operation – for example, reading information from its hard disk, drawing a circle on the screen, playing a sound through its loudspeakers, performing divisions and multiplications, and adding whole numbers (integers). We could take a random sample of computers with the same sort of central processing unit (CPU) chip, put each of them through the standard benchmark tests and factor-analyse the results. Computers differ in the quality of their hardware. Some have fast disk drives; others have slow ones. Some have good graphics cards that allow them to put shapes on the screen very quickly; others are slower. And, of course, the speed of their CPU chips will vary. So if these results were factor-analysed a diagram rather similar to that in Figure One would be obtained. All the benchmark tests that reflect the performance of the graphics card would form one factor (rather like the second-order abilities in the figure). The tests that reflect the ability of the chip to perform multiplications and divisions would form another, and so on. And at the level above this, the speed of the CPU will influence everything, so there will be a g factor – computers with slower CPUs will generally be slower at all the benchmark tests.

The hierarchical model of abilities outlined above is certainly consistent with the idea that there may be something about individuals, analogous to the 'CPU speed' of the computer, which determines how well they will perform on just about every task that requires thought, although each person will also show specific strengths and weaknesses as indicated by the primary and second-order factors. Most current research in intelligence tries to understand what it is that causes these factors to emerge. For example, is the g factor influenced by our childhood experiences – the sorts of environmental stimulation that we receive in our early years? Might it reflect some properties of the nerve cells in the brain? Are our verbal skills intimately linked with the speed at which our brains can encode and retrieve the meaning of words? Some of this work will be considered in Chapter 8.

Gardner and Goleman: two popular theories

Two other theories of intelligence are currently popular – although, in my view, each is poorly supported by empirical evidence and unable to add much to our understanding of the nature of human abilities as shown in the hierarchical model in Figure One. However, if I omit them some readers are bound to complain! The first is the Harvard educationalist Howard Gardner's theory of multiple intelligences.[5] In *Frames of Mind* (1993) he rejected factor analysis as a tool for exploring the structure of abilities. Instead he performed a literature search, looking for empirical evidence of various behaviours which:

> Appear at the same time during development
> Have their own system of symbols
> Are affected in similar ways by drugs, brain damage, etc
> Are culturally valued
> Appear together in prodigies, idiots, savants
> Interfere with each other (rather like rubbing one's stomach whilst patting one's head)
> Transfer, so that practice on one task improves performance on another
> Have already been identified in the literature (!)

By following this approach Gardner aimed to identify groups of behaviours – he calls them 'intelligences' – which have the same biological or social origins. He came up with a list of eight such 'intelligences': language, music, logical/mathematical, spatial, bodily kinaesthetic, interpersonal, intrapersonal and naturalist. The first four are fairly obvious. In the last four, bodily/kinaesthetic intelligence reflects grace and poise, interpersonal is to do with social skills, intrapersonal is about recognizing one's own emotions and needs, and naturalist is to do with sensitivity to the natural world. But the list is probably not complete. For example, where is sexual intelligence? A whole range of sexual behaviours start at puberty, are valued by society, have their own symbols and are influenced by drugs, etc. So why is there no factor of sexual intelligence? Also, the last four 'intelligences' do not really fall within the definition of *mental* abilities given in the previous chapter. Furthermore, the first four abilities identified by Gardner seem to correspond closely to mental abilities previously identified by John Carroll, Louis Thurstone and others. So my view is that Gardner's basic model is entirely consistent with what has gone before, rather than being anything novel or revolutionary.

There is, however, one issue where I believe that Gardner's claims are completely incorrect. He assumes (without a scrap of empirical evidence) that the eight intelligences are independent of each other. This flies in the face of a century's research which shows that *all* abilities tend to be correlated, quite substantially – people who are well below average in one area very rarely excel in others. This is a well-substantiated empirical fact which Gardner chooses to ignore.

Gardner's theories have received almost no coverage in the psychological journals, but educators have seized upon them with enthusiasm. For if Gardner was correct, and the various 'intelligences' are indeed independent, then every child is likely to have some strengths that can be developed in school. So what if Jane's mathematical/logical skills are mediocre? She may excel in interpersonal or bodily/kinaesthetic intelligence, or one of the other intelligences, and the school system should play to the individual child's strengths. I could not agree more with this sentiment – but given that the evidence shows that children who perform well below average in one area are unlikely to excel in others, it is difficult to see how it can possibly work in practice.

Emotional intelligence

The notion of emotional intelligence has also been heavily promoted in recent years, both for children and adults (particularly managers). According to D. Goleman (a journalist with a PhD in Psychology who popularized the topic in the 1990s), emotional intelligence can 'matter more than IQ' when predicting effectiveness in the workplace.[6] The message is that managers and employees who are sensitive to their own emotional needs and the needs of others are likely to get on better in life and the workplace than some emotionally deprived (but highly intelligent) monster.

The problem is that different psychologists mean quite different things by 'emotional intelligence', and it is not entirely clear that it is distinct from some existing personality characteristics. The first way of assessing it involves determining whether people can, in fact, recognize which emotions others experience. They may be shown pictures or videos, and asked to decide what the people in these images are feeling. However, most of the research is based on questionnaires that ask about emotional sensitivity: 'Do you find it easy to tune in to other people's feelings?', and so on. It has been found that there is little or no overlap between a person's ability to recognize emotions in others and his or her self-report – many of those who claim to be sensitive are not able to recognize emotions, and vice versa. There are also some substantial overlaps between scores on these self-reports and existing personality scales. Thus emotional intelligence as assessed by self-report may not be a 'new' phenomenon at all. So at present it seems that the questionnaires that are supposed to measure this wonderful new ability simply measure personality characteristics that have already been studied in some detail. There may well be some merit in assessing how accurately people can read others' emotional states, but most work so far has been based instead on questionnaires.

The hierarchical model of abilities has been tested and modified for almost a hundred years, and there is now general agreement amongst researchers that it lays out the relationships between the major human abilities. It can never aspire to being totally comprehensive, as it is always possible to expand the model from the bottom by including more tests to measure ever more exotic primary mental abilities: the ability to identify subtle nuances of flavour or smell, or to learn foreign languages, for example. But there is little doubt that the eight second-order factors and general intelligence adequately explain the relationships between those primary mental abilities that were thought to be most important in education and work. This is important because it tells us what to do with the scores obtained from ability tests. The finding that g sits at the top of the hierarchy tells us that it is perfectly legitimate to add together scores on a huge range of items in order to estimate a person's overall level of general intelligence, just as Binet and others assumed. (Strictly speaking, rather than simply adding the items, some statistical manipulations should first be done to ensure that (a) equal weight is given to each section – verbal, numerical, spatial, etc. – and (b) the spread of scores is the same in each section. But in practice this is unlikely to make much difference as long as the number of items in each section is similar.) The second possibility is to construct a profile of abilities based on the eight second-order factors – although there will be substantial correlations between these abilities, implying that someone who performs well below average on several of them is unlikely to excel on the others. Or we could look at the primary mental abilities, where the same thing applies.

These conclusions are based on the huge amount of hard data collected since the early years of the twentieth century and reanalysed by Carroll during the 1990s. There is always a tendency to favour a new theory over an old one, but the amount of popular attention devoted to multiple intelligence theory and the notion of emotional intelligence seems both surprising and alarming, given that both these theories simply do not appear to fit the observed facts particularly well. The notion of general intelligence is venerable, but it is probably also correct.

But how can we compare people who sat different tests, varying the number of items and their difficulty? The answer is via the idea of IQ, which is discussed in the next chapter.

Summary

This chapter has shown how views about the structure of abilities have changed over time. In the nineteenth century it was assumed (without evidence) that people would perform at a similar level when solving all problems that require thought, and Spearman's work suggested that this was so. We now know that we can describe people's reasoning in terms of a single general intelligence factor (g), eight second-order abilities or more than 50 primary mental abilities.

Chapter 3

Interpreting test scores

The previous chapters discuss how psychological tests work, and we have seen that factor analysis shows it is perfectly legitimate to add up people's scores on a wide variety of different test items in order to assess their level of general ability (g). What has not yet been discussed is how to make sense of the scores that are obtained from such tests. Suppose that two people have been given two different tests measuring general ability. One person sat a 100-item test, the other a 150-item one. The first person scored 70 out of 100; the second 50 out of 150. Who is the more intelligent? As it stands it is impossible to tell. It all depends on how difficult the items in the two tests were. The 100-item test may have been very easy, so that almost everyone would have scored over 70, and the 150-item one may have been exceptionally difficult, so that only 1% or so of people would have scored more than 50. In order to compare scores from different tests that vary in difficulty and length, it is necessary to compare a person's total score on a particular test with the scores obtained by other people in the population who sit the same test. Only then can we interpret them.

Some of the material in this chapter is a little more mathematical than usual – but as it examines ways to interpret test scores it is difficult to avoid this. All you need to remember is that it is possible to translate the score from any test into a measure of IQ (although traditionally this is usually done for tests measuring general ability, *g*). The average IQ for a particular age group is always exactly 100 and about two-thirds of any population has an IQ between 85 and 115, and 95% has an IQ between 70 and 130. For details of how and why the concept of IQ was devised, how test scores are translated into IQs and how IQs are interpreted, read on.

There are two main methods for comparing people who have taken different tests like the 100-item and 150-item ones described above. Both methods require that the test is first administered to a large, random sample of the population. The population is whichever group against which one wants to measure a person's performance. We *usually* want to compare a person's score with all the inhabitants of a country, but it would be quite legitimate (for example) to compare a student with all other students of the same age attending the same school or college. However we define the population, great care must be taken to obtain a true cross-section of people to test. Recruiting this sample is no easy matter. It must resemble the population in terms of gender, geographical location, urban/rural setting, social class and ethnic background – just to ensure that it mirrors the population as a whole. The people in the sample, recruited by market-research agencies, are given the test under its standard conditions and if the sample is large (several hundred), and has been correctly recruited, the proportion of people who obtain a particular score on the test should closely resemble the proportion that would have got that score if the test had been administered to everyone in the country.

Tables of norms

Test scores obtained in this way are called 'norms'. All intelligence tests have a table like the one in Figure Two (opposite) that shows the proportion of the people tested who obtain each particular score in the test. The first column of the table shows all the possible scores that people could have obtained on this test. These range from 0 to 17 as there were 17 items, with each item answered correctly receiving one point and each item answered incorrectly receiving zero points. The second column shows how many people obtained each particular score – for example, 352 people got a score of exactly 6. The third column divides each entry in the second column by the number of people in the sample (2979 in this example) to show the proportion of people who obtained each score. If the sample of 2979 people is large enough and representative of everyone in the population, the proportions shown in the third column should be close to the proportions we would get if the test was given to everyone in the country, instead of just the sample of 2979 people. The fourth column shows the proportion of people who obtained each score *or lower*. So if 0.005 of the sample score zero on the test and 0.013 of the sample score 1, the proportion scoring 1 or less will be 0.005 + 0.013 = 0.018. All reputable ability tests will report a table something like this one, for without it there is no way of making sense of an individual's score.

To interpret a person's score it is first necessary to assume that he or she is a member of the population being tested. It is important to recognize that this assumption is being made. For example, if the test data shown in the table were gathered from adults in the USA, it would be inappropriate to use the table to determine the mental ability of an immigrant tested at the port

Total Score	Number of people with this score	Proportion of people with this score	Proportion with this score or lower	IQ with sd=15
0	17	0.005	0.005	62
1	38	0.013	0.018	69
2	74	0.025	0.043	74
3	129	0.043	0.087	80
4	201	0.067	0.154	85
5	281	0.094	0.248	90
6	352	0.118	0.367	95
7	393	0.132	0.498	100
8	393	0.132	0.630	105
9	352	0.118	0.749	110
10	281	0.094	0.843	115
11	201	0.067	0.910	120
12	129	0.043	0.954	125
13	74	0.025	0.979	130
14	38	0.013	0.991	136
15	17	0.006	0.997	141
16	7	0.002	0.999	148
17	2	0.001	1.000	
Total	2979	0	1	

Scores obtained on a hypothetical ability test by a sample of 2979 people, carefully sampled from the general population.

Figure Two

of entry, whose lack of the necessary language skills or background knowledge may mean that the test is not able to show their true ability. Regrettably, tests were used like this in the United States in the 1920s – an appalling procedure which gave the mental-testing movement a bad name.

However, if a person is a member of the population that was sampled in the table, all that has to be done in order to interpret his or her test score is to look at the fourth column. This shows, for example, that if a person scored 4 out of 17 on the test, only about 15% (0.154) of the population performed this badly or

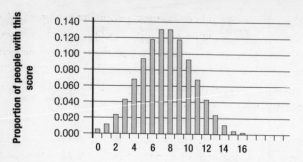

Test scores from Figure Two.

Figure Three

worse: the person is in the bottom 15% or so of the population. About 50% of the sample scored 7 or below, so a score of 7 would be interpreted as showing an average level of ability. 95.4% (call it 95%) of the sample scored 12 or less. Therefore 100 minus 95 (5%) will have scored 13 or above. So someone with a score of 13 is in the top 5% of the population.

This approach gets round the problem noted at the start of this chapter – making sense of 'raw' test scores. (Is someone who scored 70 out of 100 on one test for general ability any more or less intelligent that someone who scored 50 out of 150 on another one, also measuring general ability?). To answer this question, all that is necessary is to look at the tables of norms for the two tests that measure the same ability. These may, for example, reveal that 40% of people scored 70 or less on the 100-item test, whereas 60% scored 50 or less on the 150-item test. So it would seem that the person who scored 50 on the 150-item test would be more able. That test was obviously a hard one!

The good thing about this method of interpreting test scores is that it makes no assumptions whatsoever about the number of hard, medium-difficulty or easy items in the test. However, it does require the use of a very large sample to ensure that there are reasonable numbers of people with scores at the extremes of the scale otherwise the test will not produce accurate results for people with extremely low (or extremely high) abilities. This is because most people have scores that are close to average. In Figure 3.1a, only 7 people out of 2979 score 16, whilst 393 score 7. If only a few people in the sample have a particular score, we cannot be confident that the proportion of people with that score in the sample will be the same as the proportion who have it in the population.

Age and performance on tests

Performance on all tests of mental abilities tends to rise during childhood, and the increase slows down in late adolescence so that people are at their peak in their mid-20s. (Interestingly, it has been known for years that research mathematicians do their best work during their 20s; by the time they are 30 they are 'over the hill' as far as their research output is concerned.) For one reason or another older people perform less and less well, particularly after the age of about 55, and particularly when solving problems that require reasoning. Access to knowledge (including vocabulary, etc.) is slightly less badly affected by age.

These issues are discussed in more detail in Chapter 4, but I mention them here because of their implications for interpreting a person's test score. It would obviously be crazy to compare a six-year-old child's score on a test with those obtained by nine-year old children, adults or a mixture of children aged between six and nine. As there is a steady growth in mental ability throughout childhood it will probably be the case that all the nine-year-olds will perform better than any of the six-year-olds. It only makes sense to compare a child with his or her peers: that is, children of a similar age. Some of the best tests (the Wechsler Intelligence Scale for Children, for example) show scores for each three-month period during childhood. A separate table, rather like Figure Two, is produced for children aged between six years and a day and six years and three months, there is another for children aged six years three months and a day to six years and six months, and so on. The width of the interval reflects the amount of change in test scores that typically occurs within that period. Thus, during childhood a three-month interval is probably sensible. During adolescence (when the rate of improvement slows) six- or 12-month intervals will probably suffice, during late adolescence and early adulthood the interval could span five years or more, and during the 'plateau' period after the mid-20s it could be still longer.

The two meanings of IQ

The term 'Intelligence Quotient' or IQ was coined during the 1920s to describe a child's level of performance on tests of general intelligence. Confusingly, it has two quite different meanings. The first is only applicable to children (and even then makes some fairly unlikely assumptions) and compares a child's performance to those of children of different ages. The flaws in this definition of IQ were recognized by the 1940s, but teachers and the general public had got used to the term. So rather than abandon it, the term was redefined in a way that avoided all the problems of the old definition, and which also meant that it was possible to use the term to describe the level of general intelligence in adults. The earlier, obsolete, definition is properly called 'ratio IQ', the modern definition is known as the 'deviation IQ'.

Ratio IQ

During the early years of ability testing, psychologists and teachers tried out a number of techniques for comparing the general mental ability of children. If it is assumed that there is a steady increase in mental ability from month to month during childhood, and that this is reflected in the scores obtained on the test (two really major assumptions!), it is possible to compare a child's performance on an ability test with those of younger or older children to determine whether the child is precocious, or whether his or her mental abilities are somewhat lower than one would expect for their age. There is no reason at all why this could not be done using tables of norms, as shown. Indeed, as this approach avoids having to assume anything about the rate of developmental change or whether it is precisely mirrored in the test score, it would be the preferred solution from a statistical point of view. But, for whatever reason, psychologists instead calculated something called the 'ratio IQ'.

Suppose that the same test has been given to children of different ages. It might be found that the average score obtained by children aged 72 months is 50 items correct, the average for those aged 78 months is 55 correct, and the average for 84-month-old children is 60 correct.

Suppose that a psychologist now wants to assess the performance of a single child, aged 78 months. 78 months is the child's *chronological age* (CA). Suppose that this child is given the test and obtains a score of 60. By looking at the average scores obtained by various age groups, the psychologist would notice that a score of 60 is usually obtained by children aged 84 months. So the *mental age* (MA) of this 78-month-old child is 84 months. Given a child's mental age and chronological age, ratio IQ is defined as:

Ratio IQ = (MA × 100) ÷ CA
In this case (84 × 100) ÷ 78, or 108.

If an 84-month-old child had performed at the level of the average 72-month-old, their ratio IQ would be 86, as you may care to verify. A ratio IQ of 100 indicates that a child is performing at an average level for their age; one above 100 that he or she is performing better than average and one below 100 that they are performing worse than average for their age.

However, this definition of IQ is flawed for three reasons and it should never, ever, be used. First, it is necessary to assume that there is a steady, year-on-year increase in the mental abilities of children. But we know this is not the case; although test scores rise steadily with age from the age of about four years to about ten years, the rate of increase slows in adolescence. Second, how can this definition be used with adults? Suppose that the average score of 25-year-olds on a test is 60, and the average scores of all younger and older age groups are less than this (as abilities peak in the 20s). How can we calculate the ratio IQ of a 25-year-old who scores 65 on the test? As no older age group has an average score this high it cannot be done. Finally, how much deviation on either side of the age-norm is 'normal'? It may be the case that there is a bigger range of scores on a test at some ages rather than others – for example, the 78-month-olds may score between 45 and 65 (a range of 20 points) whereas the 84-month-olds may score between 55 and 65 (a range of 10 points). It is much more 'normal' for a child to be 5 points below the average for their age if they are 78 months old rather than 84 months. But the definition of ratio IQ cannot take this into account. So, for these three reasons the term fell into decline, and was replaced by the deviation IQ.

Deviation IQ

The idea of the deviation IQ is closely linked to the tables of norms discussed above. Figure Three plots the data from the third column of Figure Two as a graph. It shows the proportion of people obtaining each score on the 17-item test. A graph shaped like this is called a 'normal' curve' or 'bell curve' and a surprisingly large number of naturally occurring events produce graphs of this shape. For example, if the height of a sample of 1000 women was measured and rounded to the nearest centimetre, and the data was plotted as a graph, the result would closely resemble a bell-shaped curve. There are very good statistical reasons why this should be so, the details of which are beyond this book. If the distribution of scores from a test resembles a bell-shaped curve, it means most people have a score that is quite close to the average – with very low and very high scores being obtained by only a very few people. This is clearly seen in the case of height, where most women are within a few centimetres of the average height; there are rather few very tall or very short people in the population.

The deviation IQ simply rescales the data from the table of norms so that it follows a bell curve with an average of 100, as shown in Figure Three, and the final column of Figure Two shows the various scores converted into IQs as discussed below. Within any population (and from any test), the average IQ will be precisely 100, by definition. IQs are always shown as whole numbers (97 rather than 96.843, for example) and Figure Four shows the proportion of people getting each possible IQ value between 60 and 140 – it is like the graph shown in Figure Three, only with a lot more columns (81 possible values, rather than the 17 of Figure Two).

Standard deviations

It is also necessary to specify how wide the bell curve will be. Figure Four shows three bell curves, one of which is very wide and the other two somewhat narrower. As well as specifying that the average IQ should be 100, it is necessary to specify another statistic – the 'standard deviation' – to show how closely the IQ scores should be clustered around the mean; that is, whether the bell curve should be tall and wide or short and fat. A small standard deviation means that all the scores are quite close to the average; a large standard deviation that there is a much larger spread of scores above and below the average. Figure Four shows the bell curves corresponding to standard deviations of 15, 16 and 20 – because (confusingly) the authors of different IQ tests have chosen to use different values of the standard deviation when constructing their tests. (As if life was not complicated enough…)

The beauty of deviation IQ is that, like tables of norms, it allows you to judge how 'extreme' a person's score is. By definition, about half the people in the population will have an IQ below 100; about half will have one above 100 (and some will have an IQ of exactly 100). This is known because when we add the proportion of people getting an IQ of 0 to the proportion of people getting an IQ of 1, etc. up to the proportion of people getting an IQ of 100, the total is 0.5.

We also know that, by definition, 68% of the population will have IQs between 100 minus the standard deviation of the test and 100 plus the standard deviation of the test. So, if a test has a standard deviation of 15, 68% of the population will have IQs between 85 and 115. This can be proved by adding together the proportion with an IQ of 86, the proportion with one of 87 and so on up to the proportion with an IQ of 115: the result will be 0.68. Again by definition, about 95% of people have an IQ that is somewhere between two standard deviations above the mean (between 70 and 130 for a test whose standard deviation is 15; between 60 and 140 for a test whose standard deviation is 20). Therefore, if you know a person's IQ and the standard deviation used by the person who constructed the test you can easily work out whether they are in the top 2.5% (above 100 plus two standard deviations), the top 16% (100 plus one standard deviation), whether they are in the bottom

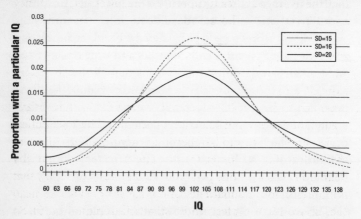

Proportion of people obtaining each particular IQ score between 60 and 140 for IQ tests with standard deviations of 15, 16 and 20.

Figure Four

16% of the population (less than 100 minus one standard deviation) or bottom 2.5% (100 minus two standard deviations), or whether their scores are essentially average (between 100 minus one standard deviation and 100 plus one standard deviation). Figure Two (page 45) shows a few more examples of how common various IQs are; see the fourth column and the IQ equivalents (with a standard deviation of 15) shown in the fifth column.

It is a great nuisance that the interpretation of IQ depends crucially on the standard deviation assumed by the person who designed the test. If you ever need to compare scores of two people who sat tests that use different standard deviations, simply calculate how many standard deviations below or above the mean the person is on each test. This will tell you which person is the more intelligent. For example, suppose that Ethel had an IQ of 85 on a test with a standard deviation of 20. Fred had an IQ of 88 on a test with a standard deviation of 15. Ethel's IQ is $(100 - 85) \div 20 = 0.75$ of a standard deviation below the mean. Fred's is $(100 - 88) \div 15 = 0.8$ of a standard deviation below the mean. So Ethel is slightly smarter than Fred – even though her IQ appears to be lower – because they took IQ tests that had different standard deviations.

It is important to be highly sceptical of tests that do not specify which standard deviation they assume when calculating IQ, or which seem to produce very high IQs. Remember that if the test has been properly constructed only 2.5% of the population will have IQs above 130, assuming that the test has a standard deviation of 15. Also, you should be highly sceptical of people who claim to have astoundingly high IQs – those in the order of 160, for example. The problem is that (by definition) less than one person in 10,000 will have an IQ that is more than four standard deviations above or below the mean (i.e., above 160 for a test whose standard deviation is 15). So unless the sample used to construct the table of norms is truly enormous (hundreds of thousands) it is impossible to put a precise figure on a very high (or very low) IQ, simply because we cannot be sure that anyone in the sample would have such an extreme score. About the best one can do is say that an IQ is very high (say, over three standard deviations or 145), but anyone who attempts to put a precise figure on it is skating on very thin ice. It would be very difficult to justify this statistically.

Unfortunately, several web sites that offer online IQ tests simply produce a result without telling you what standard deviation has been assumed. Without this vital information it is impossible to interpret what the score means. Likewise, most are coy about how they were normed; unless they are produced for commercial reasons it is highly unlikely that the test-constructors spent thousands of pounds identifying and testing a random sample of the population in order to work out how 'common' each particular score is.

The accuracy of IQ scores

One final issue that needs to be considered is measurement error. Every measurement we take, whether it involves measuring a curtain rail, reading a pair of weighing scales or assessing IQ, contains a certain amount of random measurement error. It is important to know how much error is associated with anything we measure. For example, instead of measuring the curtain rail just once, we could measure it a dozen times and take the average length. In fact, plotting a graph showing how many times we obtained each particular reading on would produce the bell-shaped distribution we mentioned earlier! And the standard deviation of these measurements, which is related to the width of the bell curve, tells us how much measurement error is likely to be associated with a single measurement.

The same principles apply to psychological tests. A statistic – called the 'reliability'– can be calculated to show how accurate an estimated IQ is likely to be. For example, when we estimated a person's IQ to be 102 it can tell us whether we can be fairly confident that their true IQ is between 97 and 107, or if the margin of error is likely to be larger or smaller than this. The reliability of a test is intimately related to the quality and number of its items. However, the technicalities need not be of concern here, except to note that a test produces its most accurate estimates of IQ when the person being tested has an IQ close to 100. Put another way, the margin of error may only be plus or minus five IQ points when a test estimates that someone's IQ is 102 (for example). But if the same test estimates that a person's IQ is 130 the margin of error will be much greater – perhaps we could only say with confidence that the person's true IQ is likely to be somewhere between 119 and 135. (Note that the observed score, 130, is not in the middle of this range. With high scores it is more likely that the IQ has been overestimated rather than underestimated; the opposite applies to scores that are much below 100. However, many psychologists routinely ignore this important detail!).

This is another reason to be sceptical when people claim to have enormous IQs. Even if the test used was reputable, had been normed on an enormous sample and did legitimately suggest that the IQ was very high there will be a substantial margin of error, and the true score could be quite a lot lower than the person claims.

Bias

Reliability tells us how much random measurement error is associated with a measurement; it does not tell us whether the measurement procedure is fair. A test is biased if it systematically over- or underestimates the IQ of members of a particular social, racial, cultural or gender group – for example, if it underestimates the IQ of members of some minority groups but not the IQs of members of the dominant group in society. But does the presence of differences between groups imply that there must be something wrong with the test? Consider a tape measure. Suppose that the heights of 50 men and 50 women chosen at random were measured. Statistical analysis of the data would reveal that men and women obtained different scores on the tape measure. But of course this does not imply that there is anything wrong with the tape measure. It does not shrink and shrivel every time it sees a man (thereby overestimating his height) or stretch out when measuring a woman (thereby underestimating hers). No, the tape measure reflects a true group difference. All measurement specialists agree that just because different groups obtain different scores on a test it does not *necessarily* follow that there is anything wrong with the test. There may be a genuine difference in group ability – for example, the slightly better spatial ability of men and the slightly better verbal skills of women.

Also, it is difficult to separate the issue of bias from a particular application that uses tests. In *The Science and Politics of IQ* (1974) L.J. Kamin describes how IQ tests were administered to American immigrants in the 1920s.[1] As many of them did not have English as their first tongue and knew little about American culture, of course they did appallingly badly. The test underestimated their IQs and so was biased. But the same test would probably be fine if used as part of an employment-screening process for second- or third-generation Americans. So there are not just 'good tests' and 'bad tests' – bias can arise when good tests are used inappropriately.

It is not difficult to check whether a test is biased for a particular application. All one has to do is look at the relationship between the test scores and performance for members of majority and minority groups. It might be the case that members of minority groups (for example, immigrants) with particular test scores perform much better (at school, in the workplace) than do members of the majority group (for example, white Americans) who have the same scores. If the test were unbiased, the relationship between test scores and performance would be the same for everyone, no matter to which group they belonged. In the above example the test seems to be biased, as it underestimates the potential of minority group members who generally perform much better

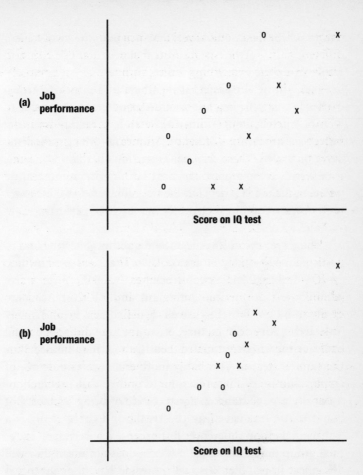

Job performance as a function of IQ for tests showing (a) bias and (b) no bias but a group difference in test scores

Figure Five

than the test scores would predict. This is shown graphically in Figure Five (a). The crosses represent the data from members of the majority group, the circles the data from members of the minority group. Both groups perform equally well at work (the average height of the crosses is roughly equal to the average height of the circles). But this is not reflected in the IQ test scores where the circles score far worse than the crosses. The relationship between IQ and job performance is clearly different for the two groups, indicating bias.

It might be the case that members of a minority group perform less well on a test than do members of the majority group – but that they perform at the same level at school or in the workplace as members of the majority group who got the same score on the test. This is shown in Figure Five (b) (page 57). In this case there is a clear group difference (the minority group's average score on the test is lower) but the test is unbiased as these lower test scores are also reflected in lower levels of performance at work or school.

There are several statistical techniques for detecting bias in tests, and these analyses usually show that tests are nowhere near as unfair as most people believe. Other more subjective techniques (for example, interviews and job references) are likely to be less fair than a well-designed and appropriately selected ability test. In the UK, at any rate, there is a legal restriction which stipulates that no test may be used for personnel selection if it shows more than a certain degree of group differences. This is done to ensure that members of minority groups stand an equal chance of being selected. But what if the test is telling the truth, and there really *is* a substantial group difference? Just because a government states that group differences must not exist does not mean they will disappear in real life! Personally, I would have thought that it was rather up to governments to ensure that members of minority groups are not disadvantaged in terms of education, social support and any other things that may adversely affect test performance once the problem had been identified. Otherwise, insisting that tests show minimal group differences is rather like outlawing tape measures because they reveal a real difference in the height of men and women.

Common misconceptions

Politicians, journalists and others who should know better sometimes end up talking nonsense when they get on to the topic of IQ scores. Here are a few common errors. It is not unknown for a politician to lament that teachers are clearly failing as half the children in our schools still have IQs below 100, or that despite a huge investment in information technology and classroom resources the IQ of the country has not risen in the past 20 years. Or that the average IQ of children in our country is no different from the IQ of children in some poor, developing nation. All of these statements are, of course, completely nonsensical. Of course, *by definition* 50% of children in the country will have an IQ of 100 or less. Since tests are normed separately in each country in which they are used, *of course* there will be no difference in the mean IQ of children in developing and developed countries. Both will be 100! And since IQ tests are renormed every few years, the mean IQ within a country will remain at precisely 100, even if pupils' raw scores on IQ tests have rocketed as a result of improved teaching, stimulation from investment in information technology, etc. IQ shows how well a child compares to his or her peers in a particular population (country) at a particular time. It cannot be used to show anything else.

Summary

This chapter has shown how tables of norms and the IQ provide a useful way of comparing people's scores, even if they have taken tests that differ in difficulty or the number of items. It also introduced the terms 'reliability' and 'bias'. The former tells us how accurately a particular test measures IQ, and the latter whether the test is fair to minority groups.

Chapter 4

Changing abilities

How much do mental abilities change over time? It turns out that this simple question can be answered in four very different ways. The first is by examining the extent to which mental abilities may be boosted – for example, by 'limbering up' before taking IQ tests, coaching people on techniques for taking tests or by 'hothousing' children by providing them with enhanced environments. This is such an important issue that it merits a chapter of its own and is considered in Chapter 5. The second is by looking at the stability of scores on ability tests to find out whether someone who performs well above average on an ability test when they are aged 11 (for example) will also generally perform well above average if the same ability is assessed again months, years or decades later. That is, we can determine whether the mental abilities that a person shows at a young age are usually stable over their life, or whether different life experiences cause people to develop different levels of skills over time. The third way is by examining whether performance on tests varies from generation to generation. If we look at the raw scores on IQ tests from children tested today and those tested 10, 20 or 50 years ago, is there any evidence that the level of performance is improving or declining? The fourth way is by looking at how performance on tests changes with age – from childhood to old age. When do we perform best, intellectually?

The stability of ability test scores over time

Most people will not undergo any special coaching in an attempt to improve their performance on ability tests, so it is reasonable to ask how much variation in test scores is normally found when someone is tested and then tested again some weeks, months or years later. This is an important question for applied psychology. If scores on intelligence tests wobble up and down from occasion to occasion without any obvious reason, so that someone who appears much more intelligent than normal on one occasion later gets only an average score, it would not be fair to use the test to make any predictions about how they will be able to perform in a job, etc. Nor would it make sense even to make a generalization such as 'so-and-so is above average in intelligence'. So if the term 'intelligence' or 'mental ability' is to have any meaning, it is vital to ensure that scores on tests really do reflect some stable characteristic of the person.

The correlation coefficient
Fortunately, it is easy enough to test whether people's scores stay the same by simply testing the same group of people on two occasions and calculating a 'correlation coefficient'. This basically shows the extent to which the scores obtained by the

people in the group are in the same order on both occasions – whether the child who performed best on a test also performs best when the group is retested in adulthood. The great thing about this correlation is that it is not affected by any increase in the scores of the group members. For example, all adults will outperform children on all mental tests, but the correlation coefficient simply shows whether the rank order is the same – immaterial of whether there has been any increase or decline in the average level of performance. The quality of a test will also influence the size of this correlation – the more random measurement error that is present in a test score, the less likely it is that similar scores will be obtained on two occasions.

Virtually all tests have been checked for stability in this way, but the most stringent study of all was recently reported by Ian Deary and his co-workers, from the University of Edinburgh.[1] They happened to come across some intelligence-test results from the 1930s mouldering in a basement in Scotland. Up until the mid-1960s pupils in England and Wales took an intelligence test at the age of 11 (the '11 plus' test) to determine whether they should attend an academically oriented ('grammar') school or a more vocational ('secondary modern') one. The same test was administered to Scottish schoolchildren in 1932 to find out the number of children in Scotland who might benefit from remedial education.

The archive found by Deary and his colleagues contained the test scores and addresses of the children who had taken the Moray House Test on 1 June 1932. After a lot of patient tracking it proved possible to locate 101 of the children (who were now pensioners aged 77), bring them together in 1998 and re-administer exactly the same test they had taken at when they were 11. (The incentive to take part was a tea-party/reunion afterwards.) The purpose of this research was manifold – for example, to relate intelligence measured in childhood to adult medical history, life achievements, etc – but here we will focus on the relationship between the test scores on the two occasions.

The analyses showed that there was a very substantial similarity between scores on the two occasions. Correlations can range from -1 to +1, a correlation of zero indicating that there is no relationship whatsoever between the two scores, and a correlation of 1.0 that the two sets of scores are exactly proportional for everyone. The correlation between the test scores in 1932 and 1998 was 0.73 which the authors rightly refer to as 'remarkable stability'. This sort of correlation clearly shows that a person's intelligence at the age of 11 is very strongly related to their intelligence at 77, even though they will have lived very different lives, experienced different environments, incomes, illnesses, exposure to toxins and so on. It is quite remarkable how similar the two sets of scores were, even though they were separated by 66 years. Nor is this an isolated study; the same sort of thing has been found in numerous other pieces of research with shorter time spans. So it seems that scores on IQ tests vary rather little over a person's lifetime – an intelligent child turns into an intelligent adult who becomes an intelligent pensioner. The relationship between the scores obtained in 1932 and 1998 is not perfect but one would not expect it to be, given that some measurement error will always be associated with any assessment of intelligence. But it does certainly show that intelligence is a remarkably stable characteristic of a person.

Perhaps it is not that surprising that an adult's life experiences, etc. do not seem to cause massive shifts in intelligence. But what about childhood experiences? Levels of performance obviously increase with age in all children, but the performance of a child relative to his or her same-age peers stays surprisingly similar. For example, even though it is difficult to assess intelligence easily in young children, and the test scores will therefore have quite a lot of measurement error, studies typically find correlations of 0.6 to 0.7 between IQs measured at ages four to seven and IQs in late adolescence. One study got round this problem by averaging IQ scores obtained at five, six and seven years. In 1961 Samuel Pinneau found the correlation with IQ at the age of 17 to be 0.86, indicating that bright 17-year-olds had almost invariably been the brightest children in primary school (and so on, for other levels of intelligence).[2] So whilst sociologists might perhaps expect that differences in life experiences – illness, the angst of adolescence, divorce, etc. – may cause children to differ in their mental abilities as they get older, the hard evidence shows that such effects are not substantial. This does not imply that intelligence is fixed and unalterable. But it does imply that, given the kinds of lives that people typically lead in our society, children who are 'bright' in childhood are very likely to grow up to be intelligent adolescents and adults.

The stability of intelligence from generation to generation

Are we smarter than our parents or grandparents? To answer this question it is necessary to back away from the idea of IQ, because (by definition) the mean IQ of any population tested at any time should be 100: if our parents were assessed 30 years ago and we are assessed this year, both groups would show mean IQs of 100 even if the level of performance had risen (or fallen!) dramatically. But it may be possible to get round this problem by considering changes in the 'raw scores' of ability tests (the average number of questions answered correctly) when the same test items are given to people of the same age who were born in different years (for example, people born in 1950 tested in 1970; others born in 1975 tested in 1995). Jim Flynn of the University of Otago in New Zealand has researched this topic extensively and made a surprising finding, known as the Flynn effect: performance on IQ tests (particularly those that do *not* involve language) rose steadily throughout the twentieth century in all countries where data was available. The size of the increase is both consistent across countries and fairly substantial, at some 3 IQ points per decade, or 30 points per century.[3] So the average child tested in

2002 would appear to have an IQ of 130 by the standards of 1903! Put another way, if a person with an average IQ (100) time-travelled back a century and took an IQ test, their IQ would be approximately 130 by the standards of 1903, so only 2% or 3% of people in the 1903 population would be as smart as they are. Conversely, a person with 'average' ability by the standards of the early twentieth century would be regarded as having special educational needs by the standards of the early twenty-first century.

Making sense of this figure is, however, quite tricky. Does it reflect a *real* increase in thinking ability, perhaps brought about by better nutrition and health care, or living in a society that requires people to process more information or solve problems of ever-increasing complexity? Certainly, some of the ones we all have to solve routinely nowadays (for example, calculating our tax assessment, programming a video recorder or diagnosing why our computer fails to connect correctly to the Internet) would have been unknown to our great-grandparents, so perhaps the increasing challenges of today's society make people more smart, out of necessity. Or might the increase simply indicate that people have got better at doing IQ tests? Perhaps they are more familiar with the sorts of items the tests contain, thanks to media exposure, and their increased use in schools and occupational selection? Maybe this vastly improved performance on IQ tests is simply restricted to IQ tests and is not reflected in how well people think and perform in real life.

It is not at all easy to find firm evidence as to whether either of these two extreme possibilities is correct, or whether the truth lies somewhere in between. For example, some authors have argued that when children with chromosomal abnormalities are excluded there are now (arguably) fewer children with special educational needs than there were a century ago, which may reflect a gradual increase in intelligence.[4] There may also have been a steady improvement in skills such as playing chess over the years – the best players are getting younger and this probably reflects a genuine increase in intelligence over time. However, there are all sorts of competing explanations. It may be the case that 20 years ago chess was played by people with varied IQs, whereas now it may be taken up just by the elite; knowledge of standard moves may perhaps be more easily available than hitherto, perhaps via the Internet; it may be easier to contact and play others of similar (high) ability thanks to the Internet; and so on. Similarly, is the continued improvement in the rate of scientific discovery simply occurring because up-and-coming young scientists are taught what was, until a few years ago, cutting-edge research, so they are starting out from a position of greater power? Or does science continue to progress because those involved in scientific research are genuinely more intelligent? The argument is not restricted to science. Whereas a century or two ago almost everyone worked manually in agriculture or industry (no matter what their IQ), and lived on a largely subsistence diet, far more people nowadays work in occupations where clarity of thought is important: we may simply get more opportunity to 'stretch' ourselves and so realize our full intellectual potential.

Evidence for a real increase

There is, however, a piece of evidence that suggests the increase may be real. It has been noticed that it is most marked for tests that do *not* involve language – for example, ones where people have to visualize objects that are spun round or solve mazes, etc. Surely, if the improvement in IQs had occurred because of an increased familiarity with test items, performance on the kinds used in language tests (vocabulary, understanding the meanings of proverbs) would also have shown a substantial improvement. Indeed, it could be argued that if increased IQs were the result of better schooling, etc. performance on such items (which are intimately linked to language skills taught in school) should increase more than nonverbal performance where the skills are not usually formally taught.

Finally, if scores have improved just because people have now become more 'savvy' at solving IQ test items, so that the scores they obtain reflect a mixture of test-taking skills and the problem-solving techniques that IQ tests were designed to tap in the first place, one might well expect the factor of general intelligence to be replaced by two factors, one reflecting general intelligence and one reflecting test-taking skills. There is precious little evidence that this has happened. The size of the relationship between IQ tests and job performance (etc.) should have declined if the tests had gradually begun to measure specific test-taking skills (which could not, by definition, correlate with day-to-day behaviour or job performance) rather than pure analytical thought. To anticipate Chapter 7, there is no evidence that this is the case. The correlations between scores on IQ tests and how people behave in everyday life seem to be at least as substantial as they ever have been.

It is very difficult, probably impossible, to know for certain whether the improved performance on nonverbal tests reflects a genuine increase in such mental abilities or if it merely reflects greater familiarity with solving IQ-test items. However, what evidence there is seems to suggest that the increases in nonverbal intelligence are probably genuine. It will also be instructive to see whether scores on IQ tests can be improved as a result of increased familiarity with the items, extra practice and so on. If it turns out that it is reasonably easy to boost performance by these means it is possible that the observed increase in IQ scores observed throughout the twentieth century may not necessarily be reflected in real-life problem-solving. However, if training for IQ tests proves to be of limited effectiveness this suggests that the increase may be real.

Changes in thinking skills with age

It is notoriously difficult to assess intelligence in very young children, who cannot use (understand, produce) language, whose attention span is short and where factors such as fatigue and hunger may affect the accuracy of the results obtained on any single occasion. Nevertheless, that has not stopped psychologists from trying to assess intelligence in young children, and several tests (for example, the Bayley scales) set out to assess intelligence in under-fours. However, the items in these tests seem rather different in nature to those found in tests designed for older children. They appear to measure speed of development rather than anything that involves thinking. For example, a child's response when the experimenter rings a small handbell may be noted. Does the child ignore it, or turn towards the sound? Is the child walking or crawling? Can the child follow a moving object with his or her eyes? And so on. Not many items in these tests obviously measure abstract thought, etc. – nor, in fairness, is it obvious how such items could be incorporated. But this means that what is assessed by these early tests – speed of development – is different from what is assessed by IQ tests in older children and adults. Indeed, there is little relationship between scores on the Bayley scale for under-fours and the Wechsler Intelligence Scale for Children (a 'benchmark' IQ test for ages 6 to 12). So it is difficult to be sure how mental abilities develop before the ages of four to six, as very young children simply do not have the basic mental skills (for example, language use) that are required for many of the tasks in traditional IQ tests.

From about 6 to 16 there is a steady annual improvement in scores on IQ tests from year to year; interestingly, this applies to virtually all abilities, with precious little evidence that some groups of skills rise and fall at particular ages. Year on year, children just seem to get better at problem-solving, and there is little evidence for developmental stages – for example, that between the ages of seven and eight years language abilities will stay reasonably constant but the child makes huge strides in some aspect of spatial thinking. Instead, it seems that children get gradually better at everything.

Quite what this implies is still a matter of some debate, and there are two main theories. It may be the case that children simply get faster at processing information – returning to the computer analogy on page 36, the central processor may simply speed up as a child gets older, and this allows him or her to perform complex mental activities more quickly. The other possibility is that children develop more 'cognitive modules' over the years – for example, brain structures used to retrieve the meaning of words, extract meaning from a sentence or perceive a three-dimensional world. The reason why they can perform better is that they can shunt problems off to the appropriate module for processing rather than tie up the central processor. Mike Anderson of the University of Western Australia (an example of the brain drain of UK scientists) discusses these issues in *Intelligence and Development*.[5] There is certainly plenty of evidence that children's speed of processing increases, mirroring quite closely changes in mental ability. But whether or not the ability to process information ever more quickly from childhood to maturity is because of individual differences in intelligence, or whether it reflects the increasing development of specialized processing modules in the brain is still unclear.

There is thus a steady increase in children's mental abilities. When it comes to establishing what happens in adulthood the literature is a little more confused, as there are two basic research designs. The first is to test a group of people of different ages (for example, 20-year-olds, some 40-year-olds, some 60-year-olds and some 80-year-olds) and work out the average score of each age group to discover how thinking skills change over the life span. Raw scores are used rather than IQs, as each age group would, by definition, show an IQ of 100. This is known as a cross-sectional design, and has the advantage of being cheap and quick to carry out. However, as is known from the Flynn effect discussed earlier in this chapter, intelligence increases from generation to generation. People born in 1983 perform better *at all ages* than people who were born in 1943. So the 20-year-olds would be expected to perform better than the 60-year-olds – not because they are younger, but because they were born four decades later! Therefore, unless we correct for the Flynn effect, it would be misleading to infer age-related changes in intelligence from this sort of experiment.

The second possibility is to recruit a sample of people and follow them up over a period of many years, in a 'longitudinal study'. For example, people may be tested when they are 20, then again when they are 40, 60 and 80. This will solve the problem of compensating for the Flynn effect – but the final results from the experiment will not be known for 80 - 20 (60) years! In addition, it has to be assumed that people who drop out of the study and cannot be traced are no different, in terms of their mental ability, from those who remain; and that when people sit the same test several times their previous experience with it does not boost their score artificially.

Conventional wisdom has it that our abilities start to decline from middle age – but as this was based on cross-sectional studies conducted before the Flynn effect was discovered it is unlikely to be correct. More recent data suggests three things.[6] First, knowledge – for example, the ability to understand and use words – probably does not decline as much with age as do reasoning skills. Second, the ability to reason clearly does decline – but there is usually little evidence of much of this before the age of 60. So as people age they rely increasingly on knowledge and experience to solve problems that, in their youth, they would probably have thought through from first principles. Third, the decline in thinking skills is associated with a marked slowing down of mental processes: people simply cannot process information as quickly as they did when they were young. (Hence, perhaps, the terrifying driving behaviour of some elderly motorists.)

Summary

Taken together these data show that general intelligence can sensibly be regarded as a stable characteristic of each person.

Clever children usually become clever adults, for example. Of course, there is a steady increase in mental abilities with age, both in the speed and the level of the problems that can be successfully solved. The Flynn effect shows that there seems to be an inexorable upwards trend in our thinking skills from generation to generation: people of a particular age now are much better at solving problems requiring thought than their parents or grandparents were at the same age. Look how easily children manage complex tasks such as programming a video recorder! One consequence of this is that age-related declines in thinking skills are rather less pronounced than used to be supposed, as early studies did not allow for the Flynn effect, and so overestimated the effects of ageing.

So far the evidence suggests that intelligence is fairly stable. But what if we try to alter it – for example, by designing an intervention to boost children's academic performance? Is it possible to turn any child into a genius through exposing him or her to a stimulating environment? Likewise, is it possible to boost IQ through practice or coaching prior to taking an IQ test? The answers are quite surprising, as is shown in the following chapter.

Chapter 5

Boosting IQ

Can IQ be improved and, if so, by how much? This is an important issue which is being actively researched. There are two main reasons for examining it. The first is to discover whether it is possible to boost children's IQ and thereby give them a better chance of succeeding in society. The second is to establish whether practice and coaching can help people perform well on IQ tests, particularly those given to job applicants or used for educational selection.

Environmental Enhancement

There is evidence that children from socially deprived backgrounds usually show lower levels of IQ than those from middle-class homes. So if IQ is (a) related to the level at which a person will function in society today (as much of the evidence in Chapter 7 certainly seems to suggest) and (b) shaped by social factors (which may or may not be the case) children who are unlucky enough to be born into a socially deprived family may be less likely than others to be able to obtain high educational qualifications or well-paying jobs. This implies that the cycle of poverty and low achievement will continue. Perhaps environmental interventions, designed to enrich the lives of socially deprived children, will allow them to perform better in school and break the cycle. For example, if children are exposed to an intensive programme of environmental stimulation, designed to boost their language and reasoning skills in the first few years of life, will this act like preventative medication and cause them to perform far better in school and in life than those who did not receive the intervention? The benefits to both the individuals and society would be considerable if such interventions proved effective.

Training

Is it possible for a person to boost their IQ through becoming familiar with the structure of the test, practising items similar to those that will be given and/or receiving training on how to boost their test performance? Examples of training include advice on whether or not to guess if unsure of the correct answer, strategies that may be useful to solve a particular type of problem and how long to spend on a 'difficult' item before giving up, in order to maximize the chances of getting a high score.

There are plenty of reasons why someone might wish to practise or be trained, the most common being to improve performance when taking an ability tests as part of a firm's or profession's selection procedure, or (in the United States) in order to perform well at the Scholastic Aptitude Test. This is administered to school-leavers and the first half is an IQ test whilst the second half assesses subject-specific knowledge. The results from the test determine the quality of university the person attends. The Graduate Record Examinations are similar, but select for postgraduate study. Both tests are produced by Educational and Testing Services in Princeton, New Jersey and much useful information plus practice versions of the SAT and GRE may be downloaded from their website www.ets.org.

The obvious problem is that if practice and/or training is effective in boosting scores on IQ tests but people vary in the amount of practice/training they receive, the scores of those who did a lot of preparation for the test may be overestimated. Those who did not prepare (and whose lack of familiarity with the format of the test items, the nature of the problems, etc. may lead to them making slower or incorrect responses) would have their potential underestimated. So, for the sake of fairness, if practice items and training materials can boost performance they should be made available to everyone or to no one.

General Issues

In environmental interventions to try to improve the lot of deprived children, and in attempts to boost scores on IQ tests, it is important to discover whether the intervention produces a *genuine* shift in the person's level of thinking skills (IQ) or mere enhanced performance on the test. For example, simply telling children the answers to some or all of the questions before they sat a test could appear to improve their IQs. However, it would only be the test score that had been enhanced – not the thinking skills that the test was designed to assess. The children who took part in the 'intervention' would not show any evidence of increased performance on any task that requires IQ; their schoolwork would not improve and it is unlikely that in later life they would undertake any more years of education or obtain better-paying jobs than children who had not taken part in the intervention. If an intervention is successful it should boost performance on both the IQ test *and on other day-to-day tasks that require intelligence*. Learning the 'tricks of the test' before taking an IQ test and fooling yourself into believing that you have boosted your intelligence is about as sensible as pretending to have lost weight by turning back the little dial that zeros the bathroom scales so that they give a spuriously low reading. The likelihood of living a longer life, our capacity to cause garden furniture to collapse and the ability to run upstairs will not be influenced in the slightest by this intervention and the reading on the scales is only important because it allows us to predict such real-life behaviour.

As discussed in Chapter 4, clever children usually become clever adults, although there are exceptions. But even if IQ measured at age 11 perfectly predicted IQ at age 77, it might still be possible to boost IQ through environmental enhancements, causing the scores of all 11-year-olds to rise by an equal amount. This would not affect the correlation. The study by Ian Deary and and his colleagues[1] showed what *normally* happens as children grow up, not what *might* happen. For example, if we understood why some children develop low IQs it might be possible to provide a stimulating environment, vitamin supplementation or whatever to boost their performance. It is an empirical issue whether such an intervention would boost the IQs of all children (making the clever children still more intelligent) or whether it would affect only the children with the lowest IQ scores.

Do enriched environments boost children's IQ?

There are plenty of case studies where children emerge with prodigiously high IQs after their parents have given them an enriched educational environment – typically one-to-one coaching at home. But unfortunately such prodigies cannot tell us anything about the link between an enriched environment and IQ. The reasons are:

(a) We do not know what the child's original IQ was.

The parents may have recognized early on that they had a very bright child, and decided to nurture him or her – but the IQ may have been equally high had the child experienced a more conventional education

(b) We do not know how many parents have tried, but failed, to boost their child's IQ through providing an enhanced learning environment.

It is therefore necessary to consider scientific studies that randomly assign children to either an experimental group (which receives the environmental intervention) or a control group (which receives no special treatment).

Several government-funded programmes in the United States have exposed groups of preschool children from severely deprived inner-city areas to either no special intervention or to an intensive attempt to stimulate their thinking skills. Some of the very first studies that attempted to boost IQ have been criticized because they may not have provided sufficient stimulation to produce an effect, but the pendulum has certainly swung the other way. In the case of one programme, the Milwaukee Project,[2] children were exposed to just about every activity (games, interactions with adults, etc.) that educational psychologists thought might influence thinking skills for eight hours every weekday, for 50 weeks per year for over four years. Children were assigned at random to either the 'stimulation' (experimental) or 'no intervention' group. Hence, if the intervention was successful, the children who received the stimulation should outperform the members of the other group both on IQ tests and on other behaviours that should reflect IQ (for example, school performance and qualifications) when both groups were followed up.

The results from the project seemed to show that an enriched early environment did indeed boost IQ. That of children who were in the stimulating environment rose to about 120 during the six years following the start of the intervention (when they were three months old), whilst the average IQ of children in the control group hovered between 90 and 100 during this period. But what happened subsequently? Follow-up studies indicated that the IQ advantage of the group whose environment had been enriched did not endure, but fell to about 105 between the ages of 6 and 13 years. This was higher than the IQ of the control group during this period (80 to 90) so it appears at first glance that the intervention has worked.

The only problem is whether the intervention produced a genuine improvement in intelligence, or whether the children just learnt how to perform better at IQ tests. If it was the former, one would expect to find the children performing slightly above average at school (as an average IQ of 105 should put them in the top 37%). But they did not perform anywhere close to this level, despite being placed in schools that were at least average in terms of teaching quality. The average mathematics score of the children in the experimental group placed them in the bottom 11% of the class by fourth grade (age nine); the control group were in the bottom 9%. Scores on a standard test of school attainment, the Metropolitan Test of Achievement, showed that the experimental group were in the bottom 20% of the class (the control group were in the bottom 10%). So although the environmental enhancement boosted the IQ test scores of children during the course of the intervention, the effect diminished when the intervention finished, and the children failed to perform as well in class as one would expect from even the diminished IQ scores. So it seems that the 'true' influence of the intervention is small, even though the experimental groups showed a higher test score than the control group and this difference endured into adolescence and beyond. This suggests that the children in the experimental group learned how to do well at the sorts of problems that are included in IQ tests, rather than showing genuine increases in intelligence.

Other studies also fail to give a definite answer to the effectiveness of enriching young children's environments. For example, the Carolina Abecedarian Project[3] followed a similar format to the Milwaukee Project, also using an intervention that began at the age of three months. Children who received an enhanced environment outperformed those who did not from the very start, showing an average IQ difference of 15 points even at 18 and 36 months. The size of this advantage declined after they started school but the difference was still there in adulthood (21 years), when the experimental group showed an average IQ of 90, as opposed to 85 for the control group. Here the question is whether the intervention did all its important work in the very earliest months (thus causing the substantial differences observed in the early months) or whether the experimental group just happened to contain children who were brighter at the outset than members of the control group and this advantage was reflected in all subsequent comparisons. It certainly does seem a little odd that massive differences in IQ are reported in even the very earliest months of the project.

Overall, it is not entirely evident that attempts to boost intelligence by providing children with stimulating surroundings and activities during their preschool years are effective in boosting intelligence. Both the Milwaukee and Abecedarian projects found that the early increases declined as soon as the children left the project and attended school. In the case of the Milwaukee Project, the IQ gains of the stimulated children were not reflected in their school performance. In the case of the Abecedarian Project, there is the possibility that the children in the intervention group were brighter than those in the control group at the outset of the project. However, even taking the Abecedarian Project at face value, the intensive stimulation failed to bring the children up to even an average level of IQ by the age of 21. Thus, whilst intensive environmental enhancements would seem to be an obvious way to increase children's abilities, those which have been tried so far seem to be (at best) only modestly effective.

There are several possible reasons why this might be the case. First, the particular interventions used may simply not have been what was required. However, the two studies discussed above were carefully designed, and the types of activity the children took part in were chosen on the basis of current educational theories, so this is unlikely to be the whole explanation. Second, the children may not have been sufficiently deprived to require the environmental stimulation. However, the research papers detail their backgrounds and it certainly seems as if they were from terribly disadvantaged homes. Finally, it may be the case that IQ is not entirely determined by the social environment, an idea that is discussed in Chapter 8.

The effects of practice and familiarity on IQ test scores

How effective are training and practice in enhancing either the IQ test score or the underlying IQ of adults? There are two issues that ought to be considered separately:

> (a) Familiarity with the test. This involves a person finding out the types of items that will be encountered, the time limits, the instructions, the types of answers required (for example, multiple-choice), the availability of calculators, dictionaries and so on.
>
> (b) Practice on items that are similar to those which will be encountered. For example, if a test is known to contain verbal analogies such as 'dog is to puppy as cat is to…', time will be spent training the person to answer these types of item.

Preparation will usually also include test-taking tips and strategies for the particular test to be taken – for example, whether or not to guess when unsure, when to decide to give up if one cannot answer an item quickly and how to eliminate unlikely answers when guessing a difficult multiple-choice question. It may also involve teaching people set answers to questions that may be asked.

Familiarity

Familiarity with the test content may be important for a number of reasons. There is a well-established relationship between anxiety and performance on ability tests. Other factors (for example, ability) being equal, people do best if they are moderately anxious when taking the test – neither totally relaxed nor a quivering bag of nerves. Familiarity with its content may well be important because it reduces levels of anxiety and may stop people from making unfortunate errors, for example, forgetting to turn to a new page of problems or marking the answers in the wrong place.

Commercial testing organizations often ensure that people who are required to take an ability test as part of a personnel selection procedure are well briefed about the nature and content of the items. Candidates will often be sent a brief test similar in content to the one that they will be given, perhaps with an invitation to take and score it under mock-exam conditions. This is often not entirely altruistic; if a person finds that this sample test is far, far too difficult for them, they are less likely to continue with their application, so pretesting may 'weed out' some of the least able applicants, thereby saving the organization some money.

It is difficult to think of any reason why such information should not be made available to those who are about to be tested. It can only improve the accuracy of the test through reducing the effects of test anxiety, and making it more likely that test-takers will remember to turn over pages in the test booklet, use calculators where appropriate, use the answer sheet properly and so on. The traditional view used to be that the instructions and example problems given at the start of most tests would allow people to see what was expected and allay anxiety.

There is some literature on how effective familiarity with a test is, but most of the research examines test performance after a person has been made familiar with the items and also coached on how to answer them. So it is difficult to be sure which of these two factors influences performance.

Unsurprisingly, increased familiarity is typically associated with better test performance. However, it does not necessarily follow that increased familiarity *causes* better performance on IQ tests, as people who seek out information about a test may be the keen ones who may have done better anyway. Studies where people are randomly assigned seem to be thin on the ground.

Practice and training

Here a person is trained to perform well on the types of problems that are included in a particular test. For example, if a particular test is known to assess mathematical proficiency by asking people to manipulate fractions candidates will be taught how to manipulate fractions, in enormous and tedious detail, and given substantial practice on these items. But *only* on these items: it is more usual to train people according to the content of the test than try to (for example) boost their performance in mathematics generally.

This sort of test-coaching is big business, and those who make money from the enterprise are quick to point out that people who have enjoyed intensive coaching after an unsuccessful attempt at taking a test such as the Scholastic Aptitude Test often perform much better the next time they take it. However, it is usually less obvious that these improvements are due entirely to the test coaching. Someone taking the test for a second time will, by definition, be more familiar with the nature of the test (as discussed above) and will also be older, which may be important as most such tests are taken by those in early adulthood. They may also be more highly motivated than someone who chooses not to receive coaching, and the evidence shows that they are also more likely do other things (for example, peruse past papers, study harder) than those who choose not to be coached.

On purely statistical grounds one would also expect some people to do better the second time they take a test. Each time someone sits a test their score will contain some random measurement error. Suppose two people whose true ability is

51 sit a test whose pass mark is 50. One scores 46 and fails. One scores 56 and passes. The person who passes will congratulate themselves, and not bother taking the test again. The person who failed may decide to take the test again, and to buy some coaching. The second time they take it their most likely score will be 51 (which is what they should have scored first time, had they been luckier), but the increase in their score is likely to be attributed to the coaching process rather than pure chance.

There is a very substantial literature on the effectiveness of coaching for the Scholastic Aptitude Test. This shows that it is possible to improve scores – much more so on the mathematical rather than the language components – although the size of the increases are not enormous, and it is not obvious whether the time a student spends being coached would not be better spent simply trying to improve their level of performance by (for example) studying mathematics. The benefits obtained from coaching are not directly proportional to the amount of time for which the student is coached. Instead, the law of diminishing returns operates. The fastest increase in performance happens at the start of the coaching process so doubling the length of coaching will not double its benefit.[4]

There have also been some studies to evaluate the effects of coaching on other IQ tests, although not many involve randomly assigning people to a coaching group or a non-coached control one. Without this comparison it is difficult to tell whether the improvements occur because of the effects of coaching, or because the people being coached were more intelligent (or better motivated) in the first place. For example, until about ten years ago most 11-year-old children in Northern Ireland took an IQ test to determine the sort of school they should later attend. They were coached by their teachers, reviewing past papers, etc. When these children were compared with others who were not going to sit the selection test, those who were coached (particularly the brighter ones who were coached) did far better.[5] However, there may have been differences in motivation between the groups as the former group knew that test performance mattered.

The training is sometimes intended to ensure that the test-taker's score overestimates their true ability. Suppose a test-constructor makes the arbitrary decision to assess verbal ability through assessing a person's prowess at grasping the meaning of proverbs. One way of coaching would be to give the test-taker practice – pointing out the need to look for an abstract rather than a literal meaning, for example. Another would be to give the hapless candidate a huge list of proverbs (and their definitions) to learn off by heart, in the hope that some of them would come up on the test. Rather than testing their verbal comprehension, the test (for this candidate) would be a test of memory skills, which might be easier. The aim of the exercise is to try to ensure that the person who has been coached performs better than they should, given their true level of verbal ability. Some different types of test items, and strategies for solving them effectively, are discussed in Chapter 6. However, there are general pieces of advice that may be useful for all tests.

Practical advice for boosting test scores

Practice items and instructions

Most tests give test-takers the chance to solve one or more easy practice items before starting the main test. One of the most frustrating things about administering a test is to see someone arrive supremely confident, half-listen to the instructions, not bother to attempt the practice item – and then discover, once the test starts, that they have not a clue what to do. It may sound blindingly obvious, but it is *vital* to listen carefully to the instructions, ensure that you understand what you are supposed to do and ask if you have any doubts. You should make particularly sure that you know:

> How to go about solving the problems.
> How to mark your answers on the answer sheet or
> test booklet.

Whether you should turn the page once you have finished the problems on it.

What the time limit is for the test or section, so that you can pace yourself.

If the test involves choosing the correct answer from several alternatives, whether wrong answers are penalized and, if so, by how much.

If in doubt about any of these, you must ask before the test begins. It is most unlikely that the test administrator will answer any questions once it has started. Do not worry about sounding foolish. If something is unclear to you it is very likely to be puzzling others too, and they will probably thank you for speaking up!

What to do when you are stuck on an item

Many tests start with the easier items and then progress to the more difficult ones. However, sooner or later you will encounter a problem that is very difficult and it is important to know how much time to spend on it. The worst possible strategy would be to persevere until time runs out, as there may be easier items just after it. If you know roughly how much time you have to complete the test, and how many items it contains, you should work out roughly how much time you should allocate to each item. This will not be exact (you will probably be able to solve the easy items quickly) but you should probably consider skipping an item after spending one-and-a-half to twice the allocated time on it. Make a mark on the answer sheet so that you can go back to it later if you have time. Then stop thinking about it, focus on the next problem and do the same thing again. Do not just glance at the next few problems in the hope of finding something that looks easy – you may start to panic if none of them look obvious.

An exception to this rule is when a test consists of several types of very different items – for example, some measuring vocabulary, some visualization and some how well you can recognize sequences of numbers. If you find some types easier than others it may be a good strategy, when you get stuck, to look through the test for the types of items you find easiest and solve all of these. Then do the same for your next-best type of item and so on.

Speed

Work as quickly as you can without making errors. Do this even if you think you will have plenty of time, as the later items may prove much harder than the earlier ones and you may well need all the time you can get.

Guessing

Knowing when and how to guess the answer to a multiple-choice test is probably the easiest way of improving your score. If wrong answers are not penalized (and they usually are not), you should *always* guess when you are unsure of an answer, and spend the last minute or so of the test ensuring that you have no blank spaces on your answer sheet. Do not guess blindly but instead look at the alternatives and see whether you can eliminate any as being obviously incorrect. For example, if you are given a sequence of letters such as A, G, J, Q, T and are asked to decide whether the next one in the series should be X, Y, Z or B, you should probably eliminate B as being unlikely because the letters in the series go up the alphabet. Some examples of how distracter items are written are given in Chapter 6. Try to eliminate as many as possible, and then choose one of the remaining answers.

It is well worth considering guessing even if you are told that wrong answers are penalized. If you can see that half or more of the answers are clearly wrong, you probably ought to take a risk and choose from one of the others.

I've chosen answer D much more often than answer C

When multiple-choice tests are being constructed the position of the 'correct' answer amongst the alternatives is chosen using a random number. You will not be able to predict which answer is correct by looking for any pattern. So you should not go down the route of saying 'I am pretty sure that the correct answer to the last three answers were choice "d" so the next one cannot possibly be "d" again'. It can. Do not waste time trying to guess what the correct answer to a problem may be by looking for patterns like this, and do not worry if you find yourself marking one alternative much more frequently than the others.

How can I prepare when I do not know what sort of test I will be given?

People often ask how they should prepare themselves for an aptitude test – for example, one that is administered as part of a promotion procedure. If the employer does not make information about a selection test available to those who are poised to take it, it is difficult to see what harm could be done by attempting some typical IQ-test items to improve your familiarity with a wide range of different types of item. Several books are available for this purpose. My favourite is Hans Eysenck's 1962 paperback *Know Your Own IQ*.[6] The IQ estimates produced by the test in this book are far too high by present standards (see the discussion of the Flynn effect in Chapter 5 for details), but the experience of taking this test is probably useful for anyone who is going to sit an ability test, if no more detailed information about the test is provided.

Fairness

If you are to be given a test as part of a selection or promotion procedure, think about whether there is anything that may cause it to underestimate your ability. If so, it is important that you tell the person or organization who will be assessing you as far as possible in advance, preferably in writing. Typical circumstances would include a diagnosis of dyslexia, poor eyesight, limited familiarity with the language or anything that would slow down the speed with which you can mark your answers.

Summary

This chapter has examined how easy it is to change IQ and change scores on IQ tests. Projects that have attempted to boost the IQs of socially deprived children have proved to be a great disappointment. Children show initial gains in IQ, but (a) these are not always substantial; (b) they are not usually long-lived; and (c) the increased scores on IQ tests may not be reflected in other areas – for example, the children do not perform as well at school as others with the same IQ. So it appears that the gains in IQ scores may arise from increased familiarity with IQ tests, and/or practice and training in the techniques of solving problems in the test. Coaching adults shows rather similar results. It is possible to boost performance to some extent, but it is harder to establish whether training courses boost IQ or the strategies needed to perform well at tests. Overall, IQ is probably not fixed, but the evidence shows that it is not completely malleable either. The chapter concluded with some practical advice that should help test-takers achieve as high a score as possible.

Chapter 6

Tricks of the Test

This chapter considers some of the types of items commonly found in IQ and ability tests, and suggests some strategies for solving them. But be warned! If you read it before taking an IQ test it is possible that your score will be overestimated. That is because the IQ is based on the test scores of a large random sample of population. If (a) the hints given here improve your performance on the test, and (b) the people on whom the IQ test was standardized did not read this chapter, your IQ will appear to be higher than it really is. So if you are about to sit an IQ test (such as the one shown in the appendix to this book) and are keen to obtain an accurate reading, you should skip this chapter until after you have taken the test. However, if you are keen to maximize (possibly overestimate) your performance you may find it useful, particularly in conjunction with the general advice in Chapter 5.

I have not attempted to cover all types of test items in this chapter, simply because I am not aware of any particular tricks that can help people to solve jigsaws, grasp the meaning of words from the context in which they are presented or perform mental arithmetic. Nor is the advice in this chapter scientific. I am passing on principles that I have found useful when devising and solving test items, rather than setting out the results from careful scientific research programmes. However, I hope some of these tips may be useful to anyone who wishes to improve their test score.

Verbal analogies

These are particularly common items because they usually
show a very substantial relationship with general intelligence.
They are designed for use with groups who have a good, fluent
grasp of the language. The items involve analogies such as:
petrol is to car as grass is to (a) lawnmover, (b) hay, (c) cow,
(d) oil.

To solve such items you first of all need to think of as many
ways as possible in which the first two terms are linked. For
example, the possibilities that ran through my mind were:

(1) Petrol is found inside a car.
(2) Petrol powers a car.
(3) Petrol causes crashed cars to explode.
(4) Petrol (usually) travels from the back to the
    front of a car.
(5) Petrol is inserted into the car using a pump.
(6) Petrol is sold wherever cars are found.

And so on. Your list may well be different, at least in part. Then
try applying each of these rules to the third term, and check
whether the result corresponds closely to any of the alternatives
you have been given. If (1) corresponds ('is inside'), then either

'cow' or 'lawnmower' could conceivably be the right answer. If two answers seem possible this probably is not the rule the test-constructor had in mind when he or she wrote the item, so you should move on and consider another. If (2) is the one being sought ('powers'), the answer would clearly have to be 'cow'. Grass doesn't usually cause anything to explode, so (3) is clearly wrong. Likewise, none of the alternatives invariably move grass from the rear to the front (only a few lawnmowers do) or squirt it around using a pump, so (4) and (5) cannot be correct. Petrol outlets spring up wherever there are lots of cars, so you might at first think that (6) might imply that (a) is correct – but this is not really a good choice as the grass does not cause lawnmowers to appear; there are plenty of prairies and moors with hardly a lawnmower salesman in sight! So the best answer is probably (2).

Note the choice of (incorrect) alternatives. When a test is being constructed these are chosen because they may be almost equally appealing to someone who is guessing randomly. 'Oil' is there to appeal to someone who thinks there ought to be another word that is vaguely similar to petrol. 'Hay' is chosen because it is similar to grass. And 'lawnmower' is included because (a) it is often associated with grass, though that is not appropriate here, and (b) it is a mechanical device like the car. Whether the different alternatives are indeed equally attractive is determined empirically when the test is being tried out prior to use.

If you do have to resort to guessing, you might want to consider eliminating words that are obviously linked to the first or second words shown ('petrol' and 'car') as these may well be put there to confuse you: the rule linking the third word to one of the alternatives will be the same as the rule linking the first and second objects, but it is highly unlikely that the fourth object will resemble either the first or the second one in any way. You may well decide that 'oil' is probably incorrect and 'lawnmower' may perhaps be incorrect, so you may choose to guess either 'cow' or 'hay'.

Once you have found the answer, check that the alternatives are likely to be the ones the question-setter would have chosen. Perhaps you misremembered the instructions and thought you were being asked to find a word that has a connection with 'oil', and you are therefore considering 'grass'. But if the question-setter wanted to know whether you understood that oil came from rotted plant matter, he or she would probably have specified 'vegetation' rather than 'grass'. As the word 'grass' is too specific, you may be doing something wrong. The correct answer should spring out at you once you find it: if you have to struggle to justify it even to yourself, then you should perhaps continue searching for another answer – and double-check that you are searching for a word associated with the third term in the series.

Verbal analogies are difficult questions to set. Items must be hard to answer correctly either because the relationship between the first and second and third and fourth terms is subtle and not easy to detect, or because there are numerous possibilities and the test-taker is therefore required to consider many alternatives. Unfortunately, it is very easy to set difficult items by making them require specialized knowledge. For example, 'occipital cortex is to vision as Broca's area is to (a) language (b) touch (c) hearing (d) emotion' is trivially easy if you happen to know the functions of various parts of the brain, but impossible to answer if you do not. This item is 'hard' because most people taking the test have no way of discovering the relationship between the first two terms. If the item is to measure thought rather than knowledge, the test-taker should be able to discern several possibilities and be able to apply each of them to the third term in order to arrive at the correct answer. It is always difficult to know how much knowledge to assume people taking the test will have. It is possible that a psychologist will want to assess specific knowledge by using the sort of item given above, for testing applicants for a particular job, for example. But this is unusual. Most of the time if you find yourself drawing on highly specialized knowledge to discern the relationship between a pair of objects – knowledge that many other people taking the test probably would not have – you are probably on the wrong track.

Nonverbal analogies

These are like verbal analogies but (unsurprisingly!) rely on shapes rather than words. For example, Figure Six shows an easy nonverbal analogy: the second shape resembles the first shape stretched horizontally. Applying the same rule to the third shape implies that (d) is the correct answer. As before, try to work out how the second shape resembles the first and apply this rule to the third shape. Then simply find which of the answers appears to be correct. If none (or more than one) seems to be correct, try to redefine or refine the rule you have discovered.

Figure Seven shows a somewhat more difficult nonverbal analogy. When faced with complex shapes like these, it makes sense to try and break them down into parts. Here all the figures seem to have one outer piece and either one, two or three inner pieces. (Is that shape in the middle of the top row a

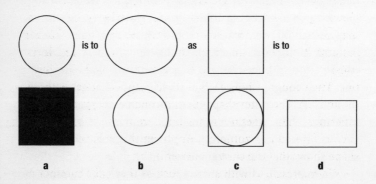

A typical non-verbal analogy task

Figure Six

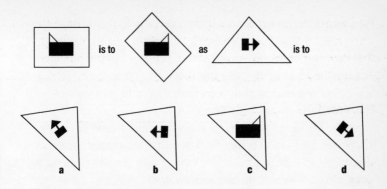

A second non-verbal analogy item

Figure Seven

sort of house? Is it a rectangle with a triangle on top? Is it a rectangle with two lines on top?) Likewise, is the shape in the middle of the third figure in the top row a vertical log with an arrow glued onto it, a vertical log plus a horizontal arrow, or a vertical log and a horizontal line plus two other lines at the tip?

Usually, in problems like this objects do not happen just to touch. So you can probably regard the inner objects as being house-like or an arrow sticking point-first out of a log. However, if you seem unable to come up with a solution you may need to reconsider this. But for now, let us assume that the patterns in the first two shapes in the top row in Figure Seven consist of two objects: the outer one and the house-like inner one. Then consider how each of these shapes changes between (a) and (b). The outer shape turns through 45 degrees and the innermost shape does not rotate but becomes its mirror image (i.e., is flipped horizontally). Applying this rule to the third shape shows that the correct answer is (b).

When presented with shapes such as these, the number of words that can describe the relationship between the objects is fairly limited. Shapes can be above, below, in front of, behind, inside, outside or overlapping other shapes. And a shape may be rotated, become a mirror image, become darker, lighter, be stretched or squashed in a certain direction, become larger or smaller from one figure to the next, or change by (for example) having the number of sides increase. (If a triangle becomes a pentagon, a square should presumably become a hexagon.) So the trick for solving these items is simply to think of ways to describe how each part of the shape changes from the first to the second figure ('stretch horizontally' for Figure Six) and apply it to the third figure: the answer you get will hopefully correspond to one of the answers given.

Many people find it helps to give the shapes a name – for example, calling the shapes in Figure Seven a 'house' or 'an arrow whose point is sticking out to the right of a vertical log' or something similar. For although these problems do not involve words, there is good evidence that they rely on language for their successful solution: it helps to talk to yourself when solving them.

Letter and number series

Number series are popular items in many IQ tests. A person is shown a list of numbers – such as 1, 3, 5, 7, 9 – and is asked (a) to deduce the rule which, when applied to a number produces the next number in the series, then (b) apply this rule to the last number in the series to obtain the answer (11 in this case). Sometimes rules are obvious, as in the present example, but they can be quite tricky at times. The easiest way to tackle these problems is to look at each pair of adjacent numbers (1,3; 3,5; 5,7; 7,9) and subtract the smaller number from the larger one. The difference between 3 and 1 is the same as the difference between 5 and 3 (etc.), so the rule is simply that the difference between each pair of items is 2, and the next term must therefore be 11. In this example the rule is trivially simple. However, this trick works even with slightly more complicated series. For example, the basis of the following series becomes obvious once it is appreciated that the difference between numbers goes up by 2 each time.

7	9	13	19	27	37	numbers in series
---	---	----	----	----	----	
	2	4	6	8	10	difference between successive numbers

The next term in the series will therefore be 37+12 = 49.

There are a few obvious series to look out for. One consists of all the prime numbers (numbers that cannot be divided by any number except themselves and 1 without giving a remainder): 1, 2, 3, 5, 7, 11, 13, 17 and so on. So if you see a lot of odd numbers, begin asking yourself if they may be prime. These could be disguised by adding or subtracting a constant such as 3, producing 4, 5, 6, 8, 10, 14, 16, 20 which would be a very difficult series to solve.

Also look out for powers (1 squared, 2 squared; 1 cubed, 2 cubed, etc.) again, perhaps, with a number added or subtracted to each term. For example, $1^3 + 1$, $2^3 + 1$, $3^3 + 1$ giving 2, 9, 28, 65, 126, 217… though, again, this would be hard to spot at first glance. However, repeatedly looking for the differences between terms in the series can make even this problem simple to solve. Just look at the differences between successive terms (7, 19, 37, 61, 91). If you cannot see a pattern here (and I cannot) apply the rule again and look at the difference between these differences (19-7, etc.) giving 12, 18, 24, 30. The next term here (following 30) will clearly be 36, in which case the term following 91 would be 91 + 36 = 127, so the next number after 217 would be 217 + 127 = 344 (which is indeed $7^3 + 1$).

Sometimes a test-designer will make the item harder by embedding two series – the odd-numbered terms will form one series, and the even-numbered ones another, obeying a quite different rule. For example:

2, 4, **4**, 7, **8**, 10, **16**, 13

The next two terms are 16 × 2 = 32 and 16, as the numbers in bold double from term to term (2, 4, 8 etc.), whilst the others go up by 3 each time (4,7,10 etc.).There are some clues that may indicate that this is happening. If numbers are repeated ('4, 4') or sometimes get smaller instead of ever larger ('16, 13') this may well suggest that you have encountered a problem that contains two embedded series. However, this is only a rough guide. Some carefully constructed items containing embedded series will pass these checks with flying colours. Another useful ruse is to check to see whether the series contains more terms than usual – in order to ensure that there is only one correct answer it is usually necessary to include at least four or five terms in a series and, as embedded series really comprise two distinct sets of terms, they will probably be quite lengthy compared to the single series you have previously been shown.

If all the tricks mentioned so far fail, look to see whether the numbers seem to get large quite quickly – for example, 3, 11, 27, 51. If so, suspect that the problem involves multiplying numbers together, or raising numbers to powers ($1^2 + 2$, $3^2 + 2$, $5^2 + 2$, etc. in the above example) in some shape or form. If the numbers increase more slowly the rule probably involves addition rather than multiplication or raising to a power.

Letter series are basically very similar to number series as most of them assume that $A = 1$, $B = 2$, etc. Recognize this and try to treat them as a simple number series (or two embedded series). Occasionally, someone cannot resist the temptation to test knowledge rather than reasoning and may include in a test something like 'Z X C V B' (look on a standard UK typewriter keyboard), 'R O Y G B' (colours of the spectrum), 'R, RA, G, A' [sic] (UK traffic lights) or some other knowledge-based trivia such as the initials of the surnames of recent prime ministers or the months of the year. There may also be separate series for vowels and consonants, etc.

You can learn a lot about number and letter series by constructing a few yourself, and noting how the various rules you apply to generate the series are reflected in the differences between successive terms of the series.

'Odd one out'

To be perfectly honest, my heart sinks whenever anyone asks me to write any 'odd one out' questions, as it is almost impossible to devise any that really do have only one plausible answer. For example, one might think that when given the series 'koala, kangaroo, platypus, elephant' most people would choose elephant (as they are not indigenous to Australia). Or should the answer be platypus (because it feeds mainly in water. Or has a bill. Or lays eggs)? There again, the answer could be koala (climbs trees) or indeed kangaroo (not an endangered species, as far as I am aware. Jumps rather than runs). Even when you think you have honed a list of words that can only have one possible 'odd one out', someone is bound to come up with something that you have not thought about – such as 'people often own these three but not the fourth' which sends you scurrying back to the drawing board. Well-written items can and do measure general intelligence, but very bright people are capable of seeing a huge number of possible relationships which it is almost impossible to foresee when the test is being developed. These items, perhaps more than any other, need extensive trials before being used – ideally asking people to explain why they have chosen a particular answer so that legitimate alternatives to the 'correct' answer can be spotted and the item eliminated.

But how to solve these items? First, forget about the physical characteristics of the words: features such as 'does not have an A in it' or 'the longest word' or 'has only two vowels: the rest have three'. I do not know of any test that expects you to regard the words in such items as mere strings of letters. Instead, you are asked to consider the objects or concepts described by the words and identify the most obvious way in which one of them differs from the others. For example, 'anxiety', 'terror', 'embarrassment' and 'relief' are all emotions – but all are unpleasant except for 'relief', so this is probably the odd one out. (Having said that, I will probably receive an e-mail from a reader explaining in some detail why one of the other answers is clearly more appropriate!)

When faced with one of these problems the best plan is to let one's mind go as blank as possible and think about the main characteristics of each of the various objects in turn. Imagine how you would describe one to someone who had never seen or encountered them before, and notice whether any similar terms seem to apply to more than one. If so, you may well be close to a solution and should check carefully whether that term could possibly be applied to one of the other objects. If it can, you have found an answer. However, you really need to rely on some common sense to check whether the answer you have found is obvious enough to be the one that ran through the mind of the person setting the question! For these items will not (usually) test esoteric knowledge, such as whether any species of kangaroo is currently regarded as endangered. You may have that knowledge, and be able to see a connection, but stand back a little and ask whether the person who set the item could reasonably expect everyone sitting the test to know that information. If not, it might be worthwhile searching for a few more characteristics, and taking into account the most glaringly obvious ones. Characteristics such as 'living', 'man-made', 'metal' (or plastic, wood…), 'uses electricity', 'found in the home' or 'edible' may often be relevant – though virtually anything could be, so it is not possible to produce a list of possible contenders as was done with the nonverbal analogies.

The problem many people encounter when trying to solve 'odd one out' problems is that they get stuck in a groove. For example, having thought that colour might be a useful way of categorizing objects they become obsessed by their visual features – their textures, shape, and so on – exploring these in rather more depth than is appropriate. It really is safer to let one's mind wander freely and produce lots of different characteristics that could describe the objects.

Remember the W words, for example:

Who (for example, who uses them? Who wrote about them? Who sells them?)

What (for example, what are they made of? What do they do?)

Where (for example, where do they come from? Where might you find them?)

When (for example, when were they popular? When did they live?)

Why (for example, why were they devised? Why are they famous?)

How (for example, how do they operate? How big are they? How old are they?)

These items can be quite difficult, and it is very tempting for a highly intelligent person to show how clever they are by choosing (and justifying, through a footnote on the answer sheet) some sort of obscure relationship that the test-constructor never envisaged. Do not give in to this temptation, especially if you are sitting one of these tests as part of a selection process. It is almost certain that an esoteric answer will simply be marked as 'wrong' and the footnote never even read. Remember that the people who set tests are basically simple souls, and give the most obvious answer that you can see.

Memory

Some intelligence tests assess memory, although the format and difficulty of these items can vary substantially. It is difficult to anticipate precisely what a particular test will ask you to memorize, but here are a few tips that may be useful.

First, it is well known that if someone is given a list of things to remember and then recall immediately, they tend to recall the items at the start of the list and those at the end of the list, and be more hazy about what was shown in the middle. (The reason, obviously enough, is that people have more time to rehearse and repeat the early items, and the ones towards the end of the list are followed by fewer others to wipe them from their memory.) Bear this in mind when learning a list, and pay rather more attention to the items in the middle third of the list than you normally would. You should also try to 'chunk' information wherever possible. For example, if you are asked to remember ten separate digits between 0 and 9 (a very hard task) you might try to group them to form larger units. For example, rather than trying to remember 1 8 4 5 2 0 5 5 9 9 as a sequence of ten numbers, break them into two or three units such as 1 8 4 5 2 and 0 5 5 9 9. Better still, try and link the numbers to something you know and remember, be they dates from history, snippets of friends' telephone numbers, house numbers or whatever. If I saw this sequence I would remember that 1845 happened to be the year my university was founded, 2055 is the title of a science fiction book, and that 99 is – well – one less than 100! Or that 18 was the number of the house in which I used to live as a child, 45 was the year the Second World War ended in Europe, and so on. Try to make the chunks as large as possible and as meaningful as possible.

As well as sequences of numbers, some tests ask you to remember pairs of objects. For example, you may be given a pageful of word-pairs to remember – doubtful cat, tranquil desk, ridiculous curtain, drunken photocopier, and so on. Here you should try to visualize the objects, making the images as ridiculous and memorable as possible. So you might think of a desk on a moonlit Caribbean beach, a large pair of underpants hanging in front of a window, a photocopier that staggers around belching out toner and singing, and so on. Some people also say you should imagine these in specific places – imagine walking down your street and seeing the cat in one garden, the underpants in someone else's window, the photocopier rampaging around in a neighbour's garage, and so on. That way you should also be able to re-create the order of the objects.

Sometimes you will be shown pairs of shapes to remember – for example, those shown in Figure Eight, and will subsequently be tested on your ability to remember which ones you saw. Again, try to give the shapes meaningful names, making them as ridiculous as possible.

Given the shapes in this figure I would probably memorize them as:

(a) A pie (Greek letter pi) on its side with a large diamond next to it on a plate.

(b) A 'James Bond' character making a tape recording from a telephone whilst sitting in a chalk circle.

(c) A pen nib chasing an arrow as it hurtles through a varying landscape, rather like a chase sequence in a science fiction film. I would not try to visualize one single landscape (for example, a forest) in case I accidentally recalled that as well.

You would almost certainly describe these objects differently, but check that where possible you remember all the important features (such as the circle round the telephone symbol) and, if

a   b   c

Three items from a memory task involving pairs of objects

Figure Eight

possible, the order in which they appear (the pie is to the left of the diamond on my imaginary dinner plate) in case this turns out to be important.

Complex sentences and logical reasoning

Several tests contain items in which you are presented with a complex sentence and are asked to work out which response you should make. Such items typically contain instructions such as IF [some statement is true] THEN [the answer is something] ELSE [the answer is something else]. For example 'if "a" is not the first letter of the alphabet then write "8" else write "0"'. The key thing is not to panic but work slowly through the sentence, being particularly careful of the word 'not'. Here if you had been asked whether 'a' is the first letter of the alphabet the phrase 'a is the first letter of the alphabet' would be true. But you are not asked for that – you are asked whether 'a is not the first letter of the alphabet', and as you know that 'a is the first letter of the alphabet' is true, 'a is not the first letter of the alphabet' has to be false. As this statement is false you do not write 8 – and so you should write '0'. In example of items requiring logical inference is 'If dwoobles are larger than twibs and plits are larger than dwoobles, are plits always larger than twibs?'. Don't panic at the unfamiliar words! I always write the terms down in order of size. As we know that dwoobles are larger than twibs, I would write:

twib   dooble.

We are then told that plits are larger than doobles. So if we add plits to the line, then it has to go to the right of the dooble. As doobles are always in between twibs and plits, plits cannot possibly be smaller than twibs. Thus the statement has to be true. Try drawing a similar diagram for 'klobs are larger than boinks. Twoozles are larger than boinks. Are boinks always larger than klobs?' and you will see that you could place a boink either to the left or the right of a klob, implying that boinks could be smaller, the same size or larger than klobs. Hence the answer to the question 'are boinks always larger than klobs' has to be 'no'. These items, perhaps more than any other, can easily fluster you if you are not expecting them. But if you take your time and work through the problems step by step they are probably not so fearsome as they first appear.

Summary

This chapter has examined some strategies that may be useful for solving IQ problems. Tests vary, and so it is impossible to give hints for all the various problems that could be devised. Indeed, the whole fascination of general intelligence is that it affects performance on so many different tasks, thus allowing test designers to come up with ever more cunning questions! In the next chapter we will see that general intelligence also seems to have a pervasive influence on how we behave in our everyday lives.

Chapter 7

IQ and everyday life

One of the most common criticisms of IQ is that it is irrelevant to how people function from day to day. Those who take this view[1] argue that whilst IQ may have a strange fascination for psychologists, and they may measure it in laboratories and clinics, the scores people obtain on such tests are clearly unrelated to how a person behaves in their job or in their home. (Armchair philosophers like using the word 'clearly' – it stops them having to go out and gather data to check whether they are correct.) The reason is that the sorts of problems people solve in everyday life – how to manage their finances, negotiate with their teenage children, even get on well at school – 'clearly' involve quite different thought processes from anything measured in an IQ test. According to this view IQ may exist, but is irrelevant to everyone other than a few psychologists.

This argument has appeared several times in print, and extravagant claims in the other direction (for example, suggesting that low levels of IQ can explain a whole range of social ills) have not helped to redress the balance. General intelligence is, by definition, a measure of a person's thought processes – how well they can think and reason – over a wide range of problems. Because it is essentially raw reasoning power (rather than knowledge or some specialized skill) it seems likely that general intelligence or IQ should be reflected in how a person typically functions in society – for example, how well they perform at work, the amount of attention they choose to pay to health warnings, their ability to manage money and so on.

Some critics[2] take the opposite view and argue that because some of the items in IQ tests do not appear to resemble the sorts of problems people face every day, clearly (that word again!) performance on IQ tests can tell us nothing about how a person will function when confronting real-life problems. But logically, the method used to assess something (e.g., heat, acidity) in the physical world need have no resemblance at all to the useful properties of the thing being assessed. Chemists may measure the acidity of a liquid by observing how it influences the colour of litmus paper or some other chemical. Physicists measure temperature by looking a the height of a column of alcohol in a thermometer. But the interesting consequences of acidity (e.g., suitability of soil for growing rhododendrons, stomach ulcers, predictable reactions with alkalis and metals) and temperature (e.g., food preservation, amount that gases expand) do not in any way resemble the arbitrarily selected instruments used to assess acidity and temperature. So why do some psychologists claim that the techniques used to assess general intelligence (the items in IQ tests) must resemble real-world problems? It seems illogical. If tests of general intelligence/IQ really give convenient, accurate measurements of how well a person can reason on just about every type of problem, in just about every setting, there is no reason to insist that the types of problems used to assess IQ should necessarily resemble the types of problems the person will try to solve in the real world.

However, psychology is an empirical science so I will not take this argument any further, but will let the facts speak for themselves. In the following few sections I outline some of the evidence that clearly shows that scores on IQ tests can predict how we perform in our day-to-day lives.

IQ and education

A huge number of studies have been performed to explore the link between performance at school and performance on IQ tests, and the results from these are virtually unanimous. Children who perform well at IQ tests also tend to perform best at school.[3] In primary/elementary school, performance is quite closely linked to IQ: for example, to a child's skill in reading, to teachers' ratings of performance and to the child's examination marks. It is harder to quantify the relationship in secondary school, where children may be streamed for many subjects. This complicates the analysis. Is a child who is 15th out of 20 in the top stream any better or worse than the child who is top of the second stream? There is no way of knowing unless both take the same examination. Also, if children can choose to study certain subjects the type of subject chosen (for example, metalwork or Latin) may itself be influenced by IQ, which will further muddy the waters. However, despite these problems there is still a substantial correlation (in the order of 0.5)[4] between IQ and performance in secondary schools.

Six possible explanations
Of course, this finding could be explained in several ways. As well as the obvious possibility that a high IQ causes certain children to perform better than others at school, there are at

least five other possible explanations for the substantial correlations often noted.

(a) As both IQ tests and school examinations rely on the use of language a child with good language skills will understand what they are supposed to do in an IQ test and will also perform well in examinations.

(b) If school performance is assessed using standardized tests (as has been common practice in recent years) children who happen to be good at taking tests will perform well at both the IQ tests and the performance tests. Those who are bad at taking tests perform poorly at both.

(c) In young children performance on both IQ tests and examinations simply reflect differences in the rate at which they mature. Those who underachieve will catch up later.

(d) Performance on both IQ tests and examinations is determined by social class, parental encouragement and other social variables.

(e) Going to school makes you clever.

In connection with (a), not all IQ tests involve language. Some assess IQ by asking the child to identify which shape comes next in a sequence, or through a variety of non-verbal tasks such as measuring the speed with which he or she can solve a simple jigsaw or create a particular pattern out of coloured wooden blocks. These tests show correlations with school performance that are as high as with the language-based ones, so different levels of familiarity with language is unlikely to be the sole explanation for these results.

Standardized tests of achievement are a fairly recent feature of school life, but the relationship between IQ scores and school performance has been known since Spearman's work in 1904[5] and shows up in teachers' ratings as well as in scores on standardized tests of school performance. So (b) is also unlikely to be the reason why this relationship is found.

As discussed in Chapter 4, IQ assessed at the age of 11 is an excellent predictor of IQ in later life. In addition, the relationship between IQ assessed at the ages of five or six and reading performance assessed at the ages of six, seven and eight actually gets stronger with age. The correlation of IQ and reading performance rises from about 0.52 when both are assessed at six to about 0.54 when IQ is assessed at the age of six but reading is assessed at seven or eight. This was the conclusion reached in 1985 by Wade Horn and T. Packard, who averaged the results from nine separate studies.[6] So (c) cannot be correct. If the children who showed delayed development at the age of six were to catch up with their peers this explanation would predict that the relationship between IQ and later reading performance should decline to near zero. If the correlation was caused by large variations between children's developmental profiles (which led some children to perform badly at both the IQ tests and school) then the correlation between IQ and verbal ability should be highest when both are measured at the same time. If reading performance is assessed some years later, different children will be lagging or spurting when their reading ability is assessed, and so the correlation should be much smaller. So differences in the rate of development cannot explain the correlation between IQ and reading skill.

It is well established that children from socially deprived backgrounds usually (but not invariably) perform less well at school than children from middle-class or affluent backgrounds, and are also more likely to end up in low-status jobs. But where does IQ come in all of this? Several American sociologists have scrutinized the relationship between children's intelligence, their social class (as estimated by the father's education and occupation), the amount of education they receive and their occupational status, and the results are rather interesting. Intelligence is, by far, the strongest determinant of how much education a child receives; and the amount of education received itself influences the type of occupation a child takes up. Social factors (father's education, father's educational attainments) are only weakly linked to the amount of education a child receives and have virtually no direct relationship to the child's occupation. It seems that intelligent children obtain more education, and this enables them to get better jobs.[7] These complex analyses also show that the effects of intelligence are quite distinct from the effects of social class, and are also much more important in predicting how much education a child will enjoy. So the idea that IQ tests are simply a sort of proxy for social deprivation – point (d) – is not really tenable. In any case, for such an argument to be taken seriously it would be necessary to put forward an explanation setting out precisely why socially disadvantaged children should have problems solving letter series, and 'odd one out' and similar items.

Point (e) is an interesting issue, as there is evidence that going to school does indeed lead to an increase in IQ – for example, when schoolchildren in Holland were prevented from attending school during the Second World War their performance on IQ tests was about 5 points lower than normal.[8] They probably also suffered other privations (poor nutrition, etc.) so it is not completely certain that the lack of schooling is the direct cause of this decline, but other studies suggest that it probably was.

For example, consider children who were born just either side of the 'cut-off date' used to determine the year in which a child goes to school. Someone born a day before the cut-off date will go to school a year before the child who is born a day after this date, so here are two children whose ages are very similar but one receives a year more schooling than does the other. Is this reflected in IQ? A 1989 study of ten-year-olds by S. Cahan and N. Cohen[9] showed that it was, particularly (and perhaps unsurprisingly) for verbal tests, although increases were also found for tests that did not use language. So the relationship between education and IQ is probably a two-way affair. School seems to develop younger children's thinking and reasoning skills, and hence their IQ. In older children it is probable that their thinking and reasoning skills (IQ) – and their experience of rewards for producing good work – leads the more able students to enter higher education.

Overall, then, there is a substantial link between a child's IQ and both his or her performance and the number of years they attend school – IQ is a stronger predictor of this variable than is social class. The number of years of education is itself related to the type of job obtained (unsurprisingly, as many professional posts are only open to graduates or those trained to postgraduate level). But the strong association between educational variables and IQ shows that critics who claim that scores on IQ tests are unrelated to anything other than the ability to take the tests are simply not well informed.

IQ and the world of work

IQ tests are widely used by occupational psychologists in order to identify which applicants for a post will be most likely to perform well if appointed. The basic idea is simple. First identify the abilities that are necessary in order to do a particular job by performing a 'job analysis', for example, or assessing the abilities of existing employees who are performing particularly well or particularly badly – such as those who excel at or fail a basic training course. It is then possible to devise tests to measure these abilities, administer them to the candidates and, on the basis of this, decide who to employ – usually in conjunction with an interview.

However there is a problem with this approach. Many organizations (for example, the military, civil service) have a policy of internal promotion so, for example, every senior commander in the British army started off as a junior officer. This can be problematical. For example, Norman Dixon[10] (an Army officer who became a distinguished psychologist at University College London after being blown up by an exploding bicycle) famously argued that the reason why generals have made many disastrous decisions is that the qualities they require (low cunning, creativity, independence of mind) are precisely those that are *not* desirable in junior officers, so people with these essential characteristics were probably rejected when they first applied to join the army. The same principle seems, at first glance, to apply to mental abilities. Those required for success in a low-grade clerical post appear to be very different from those required of a senior manager. However, because all abilities are positively correlated (someone who shines in one area will more often than not excel in other areas too) the chances are that people who are selected because of their outstanding clerical skills (for example) will also turn out to be well above average at just about everything else.

This point has been made by Robert Thorndike[11] and Art Jensen.[12] On every ability test the scores people obtain reflect four things: general intelligence; other primary and second-order abilities; a specific ability (a skill or weakness at that particular test that could not be predicted from the person's other ability factors); and random errors of measurement. Tests vary in the extent to which they measure these. Thorndike looked at a number of occupational tests and found the tests that predicted real-life job performance were almost invariably those that were the best measures of general intelligence. It is as if the thread of general intelligence that is present to a greater or lesser extent in all tests is the 'active ingredient' that allows the tests to predict performance.

Occupational psychologists usually devise different tests to select people for different jobs: a clerical skills test for one post, verbal and mathematical ability tests for another. Thorndike's work suggests that this may be misguided, and that any test that measures general intelligence is likely to perform well when used to select individuals for just about any post where thinking is important. Jensen reports similar analyses that also show that the extent to which a test measures general ability – its 'g-loading' –

Colin Cooper: The IQ Book

is related to how useful the test is for success in job training (where the correlation was 0.75, based on 24,000 people).

No one to my knowledge has ever been able to devise a test that measures some mental ability but which is also uninfluenced by g. However, the influence of g can be removed from a test score using statistical techniques. Jensen found that when this is done the tests are virtually useless for selection purposes,[13] which gives further support to the idea that general intelligence or IQ (rather than specific skills) is what is required to succeed in most jobs. However, this work is still somewhat controversial and, as the g-loading of most tests is unknown, the following is based on the simple relationships between individual tests and work performance, without consideration of the extent to which each measures general ability.

Americans who entered military service in the Second World War were immediately given an IQ test, and were also quizzed about their civilian occupation. The data[14] show quite marked differences in the mean (and range) of the IQs of members of different occupational groups. Accountants, lawyers and teachers, for example, had a mean IQ in the 120s, whilst the mean IQ for labourers, truck drivers and farmers was well below 100. There was considerably more variation in the low IQ jobs, perhaps suggesting that several really bright people chose to drive trucks, though few (if any) people of below-average intelligence became lawyers or accountants.

Of course it does not necessarily follow that high IQ is needed to cope with the intellectual demands of legal, medical or other professional training. As entry onto these courses is highly competitive, universities only choose to accept school-leavers who have high educational qualifications (and hence above-average IQ, as discussed earlier in this chapter). Those with weak qualifications simply do not get a chance to enter training. It *might* be the case that legal training is so easy that anyone at all who entered law school would be able to qualify – but because law schools only accept candidates with good qualifications, all lawyers just happen to have high IQs. If law schools decided to select people on the basis of, say, excellence at folk dancing rather than academic qualifications, it would soon be found that lawyers were first-rate folk dancers as only the best would be accepted for training! It does not imply that folk dancing is an important skill for lawyers to possess. However, there is also a literature that suggests that IQ may be important for success *within* a particular category of job, which is perhaps rather more revealing.

A reanalysis of a large number of studies shows that within various occupations the more intelligent people usually performed best. For example, J.E. Hunter and R.F. Hunter[15], then of Michigan State University, report a correlation of about 0.5 between IQ and how well a person performed as a manager, a similar figure for clerical workers and a correlation of 0.61 with sales performance. Even for lower level posts such as drivers, the correlations were just below 0.3. They report the correlations that would have been found had their tests and assessments been totally error-free, and this overestimates what would have been found if test scores were correlated with performance. Nevertheless, these figures show that IQ is a useful predictor of success within just about any occupation, and the analyses showed that scores on ability tests are much better predictors of this than, for example, job interviews, referees' reports, academic achievement or anything else. The finding that intelligence predicts performance better than academic achievement does is particularly important, as it shows that scores on IQ tests reflect more than academic attainment, a point to that will be discussed in Chapter 8.

These results suggest that if intelligence and performance could be assessed perfectly accurately, up to about 35% of the variation in the way people perform their jobs could be predicted from a single ability test that would probably take no more than an hour or two to administer to potential employees. It is little wonder that psychometric tests are widely used. Indeed, this sort of result has led one group of psychologists to observe:

Companies have unarguably saved billions of dollars by using ability tests to assure a merit-based selection process... Overall, tests of intellectual abilities are the single most predictive element in employee selection... and certainly more valid than the use of personal interviews... in predicting training and on-the-job success.[16]

Health and accidents

Are accidents always accidental, or a consequence of lower than average intelligence? Some of the evidence suggests that accident-proneness is related to intelligence. Australian men who had served in the armed forces and died of causes other than combat were followed up.[17] Out of the original sample of 46,000, 523 died between the ages of 20 and 34, generally due to external causes; most died in motor accidents. The death rate for those with IQs between 85 and 100 was twice that of those with above-average IQs, and the death rate of the few with IQs below 85 was three times higher. There was little difference between those with IQs between 100 and 115 and those with IQs above 115, suggesting that low IQ is the 'problem' rather than high IQ being a protective factor. The reasons for this are not known. It may well have something to do with risk-taking behaviour – for example, realizing that a half-second-plus delay in responding to an event will probably cause you crash into the car in front if you 'tailgate' it, or recognizing when it is particularly dangerous to tailgate (high speed, wet roads) and modifying your behaviour accordingly. They are very substantial findings, and other variables (for example, individuals' health records and their personality characteristics) were much less closely related to these 'accidents'.

IQ is also associated with health. David Lubinski and Lloyd Humphreys[18] of Iowa State University gave a health questionnaire to a very large sample of adolescents and found a correlation of 0.38 between their healthiness and their overall score on a number of mainly mathematical reasoning tests.

Whether IQ influences health (for example, through recognition of risk and the avoidance of smoking and other dangerous practices) or whether ill-health lowers IQ (for example, as a result of childhood fever damaging the brain) is unclear. But there are clear associations between IQ and how long we live, and between IQ and susceptibility to dementia (such as Alzheimer's disease) in old age.[19] High IQ is associated with a longer life expectancy and a reduced risk of dementia. There is also clear evidence from the Scottish Mental Survey that the higher a person's intelligence, the less likely they are to receive psychiatric help over their life span.[20] Quite why this is the case is unclear. It may well be because higher intelligence is associated with a greater ability to articulate options for coping with stress.

The Bell Curve debate

In 1994 Robert Herrnstein and Richard Murray published a book that caused a furore.[21] *The Bell Curve* reported some analyses from the American National Longitudinal Study of Youth in which huge samples of children were given an IQ test and subsequently followed up. As well as drawing out relatively uncontroversial links between intelligence and earnings, education and so on, Herrnstein and Murray also examined the links between intelligence, social class and social functioning. For example, they claimed to examine whether social class or IQ was best able to predict variables such as welfare dependency, whether a woman has a baby outside marriage, whether someone lives below the official poverty line, was convicted of a crime or was long-term unemployed.

According to the authors' statistical analyses of the large publicly available dataset, IQ was a far better predictor of these behaviours in young white adults than was social class. Putting it crudely, they argued that someone who is in the bottom 10% of the population with respect to intelligence is far more likely to commit crime, be unemployed and receive welfare benefits than someone who is in the bottom 10% of the population with respect to their social origins. They and several other commentators suggest that this may mean that American society is in danger of being stratified by intelligence – those with high IQs may well gain high academic qualifications, enter top jobs and earn substantial salaries whilst the cognitive underclass drop out of school, turn to crime and live on welfare benefits. It is a profoundly worrying scenario – but one that is not completely accurate.

There are several problems with the statistical analyses reported by Herrnstein and Murray and, whilst the links between intelligence and education stood up well to scrutiny, many of the others did not. This is not the place to delve into the statistical niceties, but the basic problem is that many of the relationships between social phenomena and general intelligence were rather small (though one would have to go deep into the appendices and sometimes reanalyse the data to discover this). For example, other workers have found that IQ correlates about –0.25 with juvenile delinquency. [22] There is a modest tendency for juvenile delinquents to be less intelligent than the norm. But the relationship is not substantial. IQ predicts about 6% of the causes of delinquency; 94% of the variation in delinquency is caused by factors other than IQ.

The Bell Curve did not usually report the size of the relationship each social variable showed with IQ. Instead, they compared the size of the relationship between IQ and intelligence with the size of the relationship between IQ and social class. Social class is typically a worse predictor of social phenomena than is IQ, and so an enduring theme of the book is that IQ predicts a certain behaviour two (or three, or four) times better than does social class. But to say that intelligence is twice as potent a predictor of some phenomenon rather misses the point when *neither* of them are much good. Reading the analyses in *The Bell Curve* it is easy to assume that all the relationships between intelligence and social functioning are large: many are not.

Test-score differences

The aspect of *The Bell Curve* that received the most attention is also (to my mind) the least scientifically interesting. Black Americans are known to perform worse on IQ tests than do white Americans, a finding that has been replicated many times over the past 100 years. But what causes this difference to emerge? It could be because living conditions (quality of education, health care, nutrition, etc.) may typically be worse for black children. Or there may be cultural differences in the attitude to test-taking (black children may take them less seriously than white children or prefer not to compete). It might be that being a member of a minority group somehow leads to underachievement through not expecting to do well. One study[23] showed that black university students performed well below average on a difficult verbal test when they were told it was being used to assess their individual abilities; when given the test under less threatening circumstances they performed as well as white students. Perhaps the items designed by white psychologists may be unfair to black children – for example, concepts and words are used that do not feature in black culture. Most worryingly, those on the political right have argued that the difference in test performance may reflect the genetic inferiority of black Americans.

The furore that greeted *The Bell Curve* was almost entirely devoted to the section of the book that dealt with intelligence and race. Unfortunately, many commentators took the line 'how dare they suggest…' rather than looking at the quality of the empirical data, presented by Herrnstein and Murray or in the existing psychological literature, and so resurrected several issues that had already been addressed.

For example, the literature seems to show that there is little evidence that the tests are 'biased' against members of the black community. There are several reasons for this. If cultural bias is a problem, why do members of some minority groups routinely perform better than white Americans? The items showing the largest black–white differences are usually the most abstract – for example, those involving geometric shapes, or requiring people to memorize and repeat a set of numbers that are read aloud.[24] Strangely, items that tap general knowledge (and so could be expected to show cultural bias) usually show rather small differences between groups. And suggestions that the fact that most test-administrators are white may lead to black students underachieving have been tested and found wanting. So there is a substantial difference in the test scores of black and white Americans, and some evidence suggests that this is reflected in work-related performance. The argument put forward by the political right – that these differences are biologically determined and essentially unchangeable – seems to me to be racist and deeply offensive. And several pieces of evidence seem to challenge that claim. What happens when black and white children are brought up in similar environments – for example, in an institution or by a white mother? If black children grow up to develop lower IQs for socially determined reasons (parental interactions, income, quality of schooling, etc.) black and white children brought up in similar circumstances should show rather similar scores on IQ tests. In the UK one study showed the difference between the IQs of black and white children who were raised in nurseries;[25] and, if anything, children, one or both of whose parents are black, performed rather better than those with two white parents, suggesting that any difference in IQ between the black and white children is probably socially (rather than genetically) based. Studies conducted in Germany followed up white German women who (a) had children with black or white American or French servicemen just after the Second World War, and (b) brought up the children on their own. Did the black children raised in this way show lower levels of IQ than those fathered by white servicemen? The results showed quite clearly that the race of the father made not a jot of difference to the intelligence of the child.[26] These two studies seem to show that the black–white difference in IQ is socially determined, although the exact processes are not understood.

There is, however, some conflicting evidence, such as that from the Minnesota transracial adoption studies, conducted in the USA.[27] Middle-class white parents who had adopted (a) white, (b) white mother/black father or (c) black children were studied. If the black–white IQ difference is socially determined (it was argued), bringing up black and mixed-race children in a white middle-class family should reduce the size of the IQ difference. However, this was not entirely so. The black and mixed-race children could not be mistaken for the natural children of their adopted parents, for example, and so may have been treated differently by those outside the family. In addition, except for the mixed-race group, the sample sizes were small and the groups were not evenly matched for age of adoption. Thus, although some authors make much of the finding that there were differences in the IQ of the three groups at the ages of 7 and 17, the study does not (to my mind) constitute sound evidence that the lower IQ-test performance of black Americans is genetically determined.

Summary

This chapter shows that knowing a person's IQ allows useful predictions to be made about their lives. For example, how long they will live, how healthy they will be and how well they will get on within their chosen profession or job. Several of the studies compared the influence of IQ and social class and found that the effects of IQ are still present once the effects of class are controlled statistically. So it is not the case that IQ tests are simply crude measures of an individual's social class.

The Bell Curve painted what seems to me to be an extravagantly optimistic picture of the role of intelligence in modern society. Whilst it is true that IQ shows a stronger link to various social phenomena (e.g., crime, unemployment) than does social class, in many cases both the relationships are trivially small, so it is nonsense to imply that low IQ is an important cause of (e.g.) welfare dependency.

Chapter 8

Current issues

The previous chapters have focused on the nature, assessment and practical implications of intelligence testing. But much of what has been discussed has been established for several years. Modern research in intelligence tries to answer just one question: what is it that causes people to develop different levels of intelligence? Finding the answer(s) to this is important, because only when this has been done will we have a proper scientific understanding of the topic. For example, our primitive ancestors probably deduced by trial and error that cooking meat just before you eat it will reduce the chance of getting food poisoning. This is a fact, in much the same way that the discovery that people who perform well on one ability test are likely to perform well on any other test is a fact. But science is concerned not (just) with accumulating a storehouse of facts, but with developing theories to describe why things happen. Unless this can be done we have no real understanding of the topic.

To obtain this understanding some sort of model is needed (in the case of food poisoning, one involving bacteria, toxins, etc.) which can be tested – for example, by looking for live bacteria in meat before and after cooking it. Only when such a model has been developed and appears to fit the observed facts (for example, that the rate of increase in bacteria is slower in cold temperatures probably mirrors the lower incidence of food poisoning in winter) can we claim to have a proper scientific understanding of the topic. So what *causes* people to differ in their levels of intelligence?

Environmental and genetic influences on IQ

The late Victorians had few doubts – IQ was all down to genetic make-up. Just as the characteristics of domestic and farm animals were carefully laid down through selective breeding, so too were the working classes inherently incapable of any task that required deep, analytic reasoning. (When one reads about some of the military and political debacles of the time one also wonders whether the upper classes showed much in the way of intelligence either, but that is another issue.) According to this view, the potential to show high IQ is determined by the genes people inherit from their parents, although the extent to which this potential is fulfilled will depend on the environment. A child who never attends school or learns to read or write would probably have difficulty solving many of the problems in intelligence tests as, even if the items do not directly assess language, many need words of some kind to help people to describe what they are shown – they may remember a shape as comprising a circle with a black square inside it, for example.

There was absolutely no evidence that mental abilities (rather than physical characteristics) could be inherited until Robert Tryon[1] carried out some experiments breeding rats. Rats can be trained to run through mazes for food, and it is possible to measure how well they do so by noting the number of wrong turnings that they make. Tryon took a sample of rats and identified some individuals who could learn such tasks easily ('maze bright') and others that were less good ('maze dull'). He then interbred the maze-bright rats, selected the best maze-runners from their offspring and interbred them. The maze-dull rats were also interbred, and the worst performers again selected and interbred. This process of selection and interbreeding was repeated again and again.

Tryon argued that if maze-running behaviour was genetically coded, interbreeding rats selected for high maze-running skills would produce offspring that were also wonderful at solving mazes. Likewise, interbreeding and selecting the maze-dull rats should produce really bad performers. If genes did not influence maze-running performance and the rats varied because of the way they had been brought up (or just through chance), then provided all the rats were reared and caged similarly, there should be no difference at all between the performance of the two groups. The results showed that after the seventh generation descendants of the maze-bright rats clearly outperformed the maze-dull rats at solving mazes, suggesting that abilities (as well as physical characteristics such as height and eye colour) can be inherited. Of course, people are not rats and IQ tests are not mazes, but this simple experiment showed that it may, perhaps, be possible to inherit IQ.

A huge amount of research in the twentieth century tried to determine the extent to which IQs are influenced by:

(a) The genes people inherit from their parents.
(b) The environment in which they are brought up – for example, their parents' attitudes to education, the family

income, nutrition, the availability of books and other resources, help given at home with reading and homework, and other things that will be the same for all the children in a family. This is known as the 'shared environment', or the 'common environment'.

(c) Environmental influences outside the family – for example, the effects of illness, friendships that are not shared with brothers and sisters, hobbies that are not shared with brothers and sisters, attending different schools from them and/or having different teachers, and so on. This is known as the 'unshared environment' or the 'unique environment'.

Do genes influence IQ?

Most genes are the same from person to person (ensuring that everyone has the proper number of feet in the proper place and so on) but a small fraction do vary from individual to individual. From now on, when I speak of 'genes' I refer only to the ones that vary from person to person. If genes were the only reason why people's IQ varied, one would expect a moderate similarity between the IQs of the children in a family. One would not expect them to have identical IQs, as different children would have inherited different genes and so will only share about half their genes with their brothers or sisters. If the shared environment was all-important all the children in a family would turn out to be completely identical in IQ because they have been brought up in the same family environment. If the unshared environment determined intelligence, there would be very substantial variability between brothers and sisters, since nothing they shared (genes, home environment) would influence their IQs.

Scientists have developed several techniques for determining the extent to which genes and the shared and unshared environments influence intelligence. For example, if two unrelated children of similar ages are brought up together the only thing that could make them resemble each other in terms of IQ would be the shared environment. They do not share any of the genes that vary from person to person (being unrelated) and nor, by definition, can they share their unique environments. So we can simply measure the similarity of their IQ scores at various ages, and infer how important the shared environment is at each age.

Identical twins are of particular interest to geneticists as they are exact clones of each other – they are genetically identical. Very occasionally, they get separated just after birth and are brought up in two different family environments. Some large-scale research projects have tracked down such twins and tested them individually, usually in adulthood. As long as they were separated at an early age, and brought up in quite different settings, the only thing that could make them similar would be their genetic make-up (or the experience of sharing a womb). So, by determining how similar each twin-pair is in IQ, it is possible to directly estimate the size of the genetic influence on IQ.

It is also possible to deduce the relative importance of genetic, common and unique family influences from other types of study – for example, by comparing the IQs of pairs of identical and non-identical twins who are brought up at home by their own parents. There is no space to go into this here, though I deal with this in *Intelligence and Abilities* (1999) and *Individual Differences* (2002). The reason I do not go into detail here is that the results are consistent across all types of study. Each shows that genes account for about half the variability in IQ within the samples – rather less in childhood, and rather more in middle age. Identical twins who were separated shortly after birth show test scores that are very similar indeed. Unrelated children brought up together show no similarity in IQ by adulthood.[2] The family environment influences IQ in childhood only; by the mid-teens and afterwards, its effect is close to zero.[3] Parental attitudes, help and learning resources matter not one jot as far as adult IQ is concerned (though they may influence school performance). The unshared environment accounts for the rest of the variation. This is (to me) one of the most surprising findings in the whole of psychology, but a few important warnings must be mentioned.

First, the generalization applies to the samples of children who have been tested, not to individual children. It makes no sense to say that 'half of Johnny's intelligence comes from his genetic make-up'. Second, most studies have been performed in western Europe and North America, where there is probably not all that much variation in the shared environment from family to family. For example, most children in most families will go to school where they will be taught basic numeracy and literacy amongst other things. Few will be malnourished. Most will watch television. So perhaps it can be assumed that in the cultures that have been studied most children receive the basic level of environmental stimulation that they need in order to let their genetic potential express itself. If the studies were to be carried out in cultures where some families were severely deprived, it is highly likely that the shared environment would be important. Third, just because a characteristic like intelligence is influenced by genes it does not follow that it is fixed – environmental enhancements may still be of value. The usual analogy for this is a handful of seed thrown into a sandy, barren plot and another handful thrown into a fertile plot. The height of the plants is genetically determined, but the ones that land in the fertile soil will grow higher than those thrown on to the barren soil. Finally, because genes are important *within* each racial group, it does not follow that any differences in IQ *between* racial groups reflect genetic (rather than environmental) differences (see Chapter 7).

Several sociologists and psychologists (for example, Leon Kamin[4] from Princeton University) used to point to flaws in some of the early studies and argue that these invalidated their conclusion that genes played any part in shaping IQ. However, it is now generally accepted that the heritability of intelligence is certainly much greater than zero, and is probably in the order of 0.5, thanks to more careful, more recent studies and more sophisticated methods for interpreting their results. It is simply not a controversy any more.

Modern statistical analyses also allow us to determine the periods of life at which the genes we inherit show their greatest influence on IQ. One might think that genes may be important in early life but that as people get older and learn from life experiences genes may have less and less influence on their mental skills. But the evidence shows quite the opposite. Genes make their most substantial contribution to IQ in middle age, after people have finished developing and before age-related degeneration begins.[5]

Identifying the genes

Several research groups (such as the one headed by Robert Plomin at the Institute of Psychiatry, University of London) are now trying to identify precisely which genes influence IQ. It must be said that this is proving rather more time-consuming than everyone expected, probably because IQ is influenced by a large number of different genes, each of which has a small effect. Whilst several likely contenders have been identified when analysing how the DNA of very intelligent people differs from those with average scores on IQ tests, these findings have not (at the time of writing) been replicated in other groups of people.

Because genes clearly influence IQ (and other abilities) it is surprisingly difficult to carry out experiments to investigate the extent to which parents' behaviour is influential. Consider this simple experiment. Suppose a psychologist wanted to determine whether reading to children at an early age improves their subsequent reading ability. He or she might think that the best way to test this experimentally would be to interview mothers, find out for how many hours a week they read to their children, and then follow up the children and measure their reading skills later. But this will not do, as nothing is known about the mothers. It *might* be the case that reading ability is, to some extent, influenced by genetic make-up. It also seems plausible that mothers who themselves have good reading skills are the ones who choose to spend the most time reading to their children. If this is the case, the mothers who have genes that facilitate reading will probably have passed some of these on to the child, thus predisposing him or her to show good reading skills. Thus, although there is a link between the amount of time a mother spends reading to her child and that child's subsequent reading ability, it does not follow that the mother's behaviour directly influences the child's reading skills. It may be that both the mother and child are genetically predisposed to read well. It is very easy to overestimate the effects of environmental variables if one forgets to allow for genetic influences.

This sort of problem bedevils all sorts of studies that try to evaluate the importance of social variables on IQ. Take social class, even. Suppose one wanted to test whether social deprivation lowers children's IQ. What is it that determines a parent's trade or profession and their annual income? Chapter 7 showed that these are linked to the amount of education a person receives, which is itself predicted by IQ. So when the IQs of children from low- and high-socioeconomic status families are compared, are the differences really just due to differences in social class? Sociologists usually assume so, but one would certainly expect that genetic make-up would also have some influence if genes influence IQ, IQ influences the amount of education received and the amount of education affects socioeconomic status. No one is saying that genes are the sole cause of differences between social groups, but assuming they have zero effect is common practice – and very sloppy science.

It is also known that the influence of the shared environment on adult IQ is not substantial – the important sources of environmental influence are those that stem from outside the family (the unique environment). But discovering which aspects of the unique environment are important is very difficult, precisely because they differ from child to child. If one child spends a lot of time collecting stamps, playing computer games and watching science fiction on television, whilst another enjoys playing football, hanging around shopping centres with friends and reading comics, how can one determine which of these activities 'explains' a difference in their IQs? It does not make much sense to infer that some particular activity (for example, reading for pleasure) boosts IQs after comparing the average IQs of children who do not read and who read for pleasure for it has been suggested that the type of unique environment a child experiences may be influenced by his or her genetic make-up. A bright child may seek out stimulation (join a library and read voraciously, join after-school science clubs, learn how to program a computer rather than just using it to play games) *because* of their high intelligence. So just because certain childhood hobbies and activities are associated with high (or low) IQs, it does not necessarily follow that they directly *influence* IQ level. It might just as well be that IQ influences a child's choice of activities.

Rather than trying to work out the complex relationships between child behaviour and IQ, it is very much easier to measure the extent to which biological variables influence IQ. For example, to test the hypothesis that there are differences in the way nerve cells work in high- and low-IQ individuals, all one has to do is conduct some simple laboratory experiments. This is the direction in which most recent research has moved.

IQ and Thought

Psychologists who study thinking ('cognitive psychologists') are rarely interested in why some people perform better than others at tasks involving memory, thought or perception. Instead, they usually study how some feature influences performance – for example, whether longer words are harder to remember than shorter ones, or whether the meaning of words that are frequently used in everyday speech (for example, 'man') can be grasped more quickly than words that are less frequently used (for example, 'pun').

Earl Hunt[6] spent years trying to explain individual differences in verbal ability in terms of the amount of time taken to retrieve the meanings of words from memory. One of his experiments involved showing people letters (capital and small) and asking them to decide, as quickly as they could, whether the letters were physically identical – for example, A A, B B, a a, b b would be physically identical; A B, a B, a A, b B, a b, etc. would be physically different. Then he asked people to decide whether two printed letters referred to the same letter of the alphabet: A A, a A, B b, B B for example.

Hunt argued that the second task should take longer because the person would have to carry out the extra step of extracting the *meaning* of the letter – that is, realizing that the shapes a and A were examples of the letter A. Hunt thought the speed with which the meanings of these letters could be extracted should be linked to general verbal ability: a person with great verbal skills should be able to extract the meaning of letters quickly. (Similar tasks have been devised for words – for example, by measuring how long it takes for a person to decide whether 'trub' or 'frog' are real words.) Unfortunately, however, whilst the relationships are definitely there, and in the right direction (people with better verbal skills *are* faster), they are not substantial; the speed with which people can access the meaning of letters or words can only explain about 10% of the variation in verbal ability from person to person.

There are plenty of other attempts in the literature to relate performance on IQ tests to basic mental processes, but few of them fare much better than Hunt's work. N.J. Mackintosh[7] provides an excellent and highly readable review of this literature for those who are interested. So 'explaining' intelligence in terms of basic cognitive processes does not seem to work all that well – which might suggest that there is something wrong with current assumptions about how people go about processing words, numbers, etc.

IQ and physique

The twin and adoption studies discussed earlier are interesting, but do not spell out precisely which aspects of the environment may influence a child's IQ, or how the genes that influence intelligence actually work. All any gene can do is produce a bit of protein somewhere. The finding that IQ is influenced by genetic make-up therefore tells us that we should be able to identify differences in some part of the bodies of intelligent and not-so-intelligent people. Many of these differences may be in the central nervous system, but it is common for each gene to influence several different body structures. So it *may* be the case that some of the genes that influence physical structure – height, eye colour, gender, hair colour, blood group and so on – might also influence IQ.[8] This is why several psychologists have studied the links between these physical characteristics and IQ. Several small associations have been found. Height is related to IQ for each gender (there is a slight tendency for higher IQ individuals to be taller) and it is the length of the leg that determines this – body size is unrelated to IQ. Likewise, head size and brain volume are now known to be related to IQ (despite early claims to the contrary by some authors), and short-sightedness is also known to be linked (and is not just a consequence if high-IQ individuals getting eyestrain from reading more than low-IQ people). One paper shows a small effect of eye colour on IQ. There is a small gender difference in the ability to visualize shapes (men do slightly better, so the old sexist comments about map-reading skills have a scintilla of truth in them) but women may outperform men when using language.

Reaction time and IQ

One popular biological theory of intelligence suggests that high IQ is a direct result of a person having nerves that either (a) transmit information quickly along each nerve cell, or (b) transmit information quickly and faithfully between nerve cells. According to this, some people are more intelligent than others simply because they can process information more quickly. The theory is not new; indeed, at the end of the nineteenth century Sir Francis Galton tried to determine whether highly intelligent people could respond quickly – for example, by pressing a button when a light came on. Reaction time is simply a measure of how quickly people can perform this task.

Galton lacked the technology to measure either IQ or speed of response accurately, but for years his conclusion – that there was little or no association between IQ and speed of responding – was accepted at face value. There was renewed interest in this area in the 1970s, when researchers thought that measuring such simple reaction times might prove useful in testing the idea that intelligence may reflect the speed of neural processing. Putting it crudely, one would expect a person whose nervous system could process information quickly to notice that the light had come on and respond appropriately rather more quickly than someone with a slow nervous system. A typical experiment would involve asking someone to look at a small light bulb on a metal panel and press a button under the light as quickly as possible when it came on. There are a few common enhancements, for example:

- Warning the person 1–3 seconds beforehand that the light is about to come on, to ensure that they are paying full attention.
- Measuring reaction time from the moment the light comes on until the person's hand starts to move (rather than until they push the button – some people's hands may move faster than others).
- Having several pairs of lights/buttons on the panel.

Most people are surprised to learn how long these reaction times actually are. It is practically impossible to begin to move a finger (or a foot towards the brake pedal when driving) in much less than a quarter of a second. So even with a simple task such as this, a lot of neural processing is going on.

There is a substantial literature showing a medium-sized and consistent relationship between reaction time, as measured by such tasks, and IQ.[9] People with higher IQs react somewhat more quickly than those with lower ones. The correlation is usually about -0.35, indicating that IQ can explain about 10% of the variability in reaction time from person to person. This gives some support to the general idea that IQ is linked to the speed of neural processing. A weakness of this sort of experiment is that it cannot distinguish between the speed with which information travels through the nervous system and the complexity of the path it has to follow from nerve cell to nerve cell, which may differ from person to person.

Inspection time and IQ

Inspection time is even simpler than reaction time. In an inspection-time task people are shown one of two possible shapes for a short period of time, and asked to notice some feature of the shape. In the case of the figures shown in Figure Nine they are asked to decide whether the left or the right vertical line is the longer. This feature is very obvious when a shape is presented for a long time, but the inspection-time task

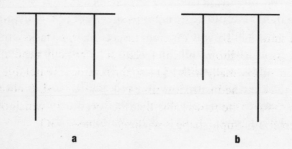

a   b

Two shapes for an Inspection Time task

Figure Nine

involves presenting one or other of the shapes for only a few thousandths of a second, and asking the person whether the left or the right line was longer. The time for which they are shown the shape is varied, and the point at which the individual can *just* manage to see the difference between the two shapes is determined. This is known as their inspection time (IT). It is the smallest amount of time that the shape must be shown for them to be able to correctly identify it.

Many tens of studies[10] show that inspection time is quite strongly related to IQ. The correlation is about −0.5, suggesting that IQ explains about a quarter of the person-to-person variability in inspection time. This finding is usually taken to suggest that inspection time reflects the speed of neural conduction – although some commentators have suggested that it may instead reflect strategy use. That is, people may do well at the task because they develop efficient strategies for helping them to identify the shapes – for example, looking where the bottom one of the 'legs' should be and noticing how much flicker there is. But this is unlikely to be correct because, although the use of strategies can affect performance on these tasks, there is still a link between inspection time and IQ in both the strategy-users and the non-strategy-users. So the use of strategy is not the sole explanation for these results. Nor is it just something to do with speed, as the correlation is still found when people are given as much time as they want to solve the IQ test. Some data recently collected by Cathal McCrory and myself show that six very different inspection-time tasks (three visual, three auditory) all interrelate substantially (and also correlate substantially with IQ) – so the findings are not due to some quirk of the inspection-time task that is used. It always strikes me as quite remarkable that the speed with which one can perceive a simple shape is so closely related to IQ.

Physiological Measures

Some psychologists are fond of gluing electrodes to the surface of the scalp and measuring the electrical activity that percolates up through it from the brain. One popular way to analyse this electrical activity is to determine how much there is at each frequency. Imagine a piano. Each key sounds a note of a particular pitch, and you can describe a complex chord by analysing the amount of activity (the loudness) and the particular frequency or pitch (identifying which key(s) were pressed). Mathematical techniques may be used to make this analysis – the sound can be fed into a computer and it will tell you which notes were pressed, and how loud each one was. Exactly the same principle is used to analyse electrical activity in the brain. The voltage from the electrodes is fed into a computer which tells you how much activity there is at each frequency ('pitch'). The most interesting frequencies are those between 8 and 14 cycles per second, which are so low-pitched that they would be almost inaudible if they were amplified and played through a loudspeaker. The sound would be more like the rumble of a distant train than anything else.

These electrical signals have been analysed when the person is sitting doing nothing, and after they have listened repeatedly to a simple sound (for example, a click played through headphones). There is some evidence to suggest that highly intelligent people show more electrical activity in the high-frequency band ('the louder the high notes') if EEG is measured when they are sitting relaxed and doing nothing.[11] The geneticist T.E. Reed and Art Jensen, a psychologist from the University of California,[12] measured how long it took a nerve impulse to travel from the eye to the visual cortex (at the back of the head). They showed people a chequerboard pattern where, every now and again, the black squares turned white and the white squares turned black. The time difference between the squares turning over and a flurry of electrical activity in the visual cortex was related to IQ, the more intelligent people processing the signal faster.

There have also been some studies using brain-imaging techniques to determine which part(s) of the brain are most active when people solve IQ tests, and whether the patterns and/or amount of brain activity are the same in low- and high-IQ individuals. Recent evidence seems to show that when people solve IQ puzzles the front part of the brain is most active. The amount of brain-cell activity is also related to IQ. People with higher IQs burn up less glucose in their brains when solving IQ problems than do people with lower IQs[13] – it is almost as if the brains of high-IQ individuals function more efficiently when they are solving problems. The same kind of thing happened when people practised solving a computer game (Tetris). Initially they expended a lot of energy (burnt a lot of glucose), but as they became more practised they performed better and the rate of glucose use also decreased. So it looks as if high intelligence is associated with more efficient brains, not ones that simply attack a problem with all neurons firing.

Summary

Some of the results outlined in this chapter are surprising. Whoever would have thought that genes are the prime determinant of a person's IQ in middle age? Or that the sort of family environment people create for their children does not usually influence their IQ beyond the age of about 14? Or that the time taken to perceive a simple pattern or react to a light would be related to IQ? We are now in a fascinating position. Geneticists can tell us whether the same genes that influence IQ in six-year-old children also influence the IQs of older children (they do), or whether the genes that influence performance in the inspection-time task are also the ones that influence performance on IQ tests (they don't seem to be, which is very odd). It is perhaps less surprising to find some links between performance on IQ tests and brain functioning, as genetic studies tell us there *must* be some sort of relationship between the two. Teasing out what it is that makes some people more smart than others is the focus of much fascinating research.

Chapter 9

Some frequently asked questions about intelligence

This book ends with some of the questions that were often raised following the UK *Test the Nation* television programme. Some of them were quite deep – for example, 'What is intelligence?' and 'My mum has a high IQ, will I?' Most of the important issues have already been addressed in the text, and for these questions I give the 'quick answer' and flag the chapter(s) in which the topic was covered. Others are more specific – for example 'Are men more intelligent than women?', 'Can you tell someone's IQ by looking at them?', 'Is intelligence linked to star signs?' – and were not covered in the text, so for these I have given slightly fuller explanations.

Where can I buy an IQ test?

Test publishers will only supply tests to qualified users (usually accredited psychologists) who have been specially trained in their choice, administration and interpretation. It is not possible for members of the public to buy commercial ability tests, though they may be able to pay an accredited psychologist (in the UK a chartered psychologist) to perform an assessment.

Can you tell someone's IQ by looking at them?

Not accurately, but there are signs. Verbal fluency is a reasonable indicator of IQ, so if a person talks fluently using precise language and demonstrating a wide vocabulary, they are probably of above average intelligence. (After getting my first lecturing job I found that one member of the interview panel had been assessing me on purely that characteristic.)

Does having a big head mean you're more intelligent?

There is a definite association between brain size (as measured by brain scans) and IQ, and a reasonable link between head size and brain size.[1] So people with large heads tend to be more intelligent than people with small ones, though head size only explains about 10% of the variability in IQ from person to person. There will be a lot of exceptions. You cannot accurately assess IQ by looking at someone's hat size!

If the average IQ is 100, why were the average regional IQs from the studio audience groups and internet-based test all well above that level?

Self-selection is the short answer. The tables that allowed us to translate test scores into IQs were compiled after giving the test to a randomly sampled cross-section of the population. So we know these tables were accurate. But it is possible that people who suspect their IQs will be low would prefer not to take the test. It may perhaps also be the case that they are less likely to own a computer, though this is pure speculation. Likewise, it seems probable that people whose IQs are substantially below 100 would be less than usually keen to be a member of the studio audience for fear that they would appear stupid. So, although the mean scores from various samples were well above average, this probably does not mean that there is anything wrong with the IQ scores.

When converting test scores to IQs, why are some age bands wide, and others narrow?

IQ shows a person's level of intelligence in relation to people of a similar age. During the time when the total scores people obtain on mental tests increase from year to year (for example, up until the early 20s) it is necessary to use quite narrow age bands when constructing the table to convert the total score into an IQ. If everyone between 16 and 25 were combined into one age band, the 16-year olds would get lower IQs than they should whilst the 25-year-olds would do better, simply because there is a substantial increase in mental ability between these two ages which should *not* be reflected in IQ. (Remember, IQ compares each person to their same-aged peers, and so the mean IQ for 16-year-olds, 30-year-olds and 90-year-olds should all be exactly 100.) For this reason, the best IQ tests for children have a separate table for each 12-week age band. But as discussed in Chapter 4 there are periods when there is not very much change in raw test scores, so it is entirely reasonable to use much broader age bands – 35 to 54 years, for example.

How accurate is my score?

It is impossible to be certain about this as we do not know the conditions under which the test was taken. If it was taken after eating a heavy meal, drinking several glasses of wine or beer in a room where other people were shouting out the answers (or making you feel nervous), and where there was a lot of noise and distraction, of course the score will be virtually meaningless. But we do know how much error is likely to be associated with the score if you took the test under ideal conditions: alert, in a quiet room with no distractions. The reliability of the test is a statistic showing how much measurement error is associated with the test scores. It allows you to construct what are known as 'confidence intervals' – so (for example) if you scored 100 on the UK version of the test (which had a reliability of 0.85) there is a 95% chance that your true score will be between 88 and 112. If your estimated IQ was 120, it is 95% likely to 'really' be between 105 and 129 etc. – see page 189. Note that the range of 'possible' scores is not the same on either side of your observed score. These margins of error are actually the same sort of size as in many commercially published tests.

My IQ was measured previously and was rather different to that measured on 'Test the Nation'. Why?

There are many possible reasons for a discrepancy in IQ test scores.

(a) The other test used a different definition of IQ. The UK version of the test used the usual definition of IQ – that is, for any age group the average score was 100, and 95% of the population score between 70 and 130. Other tests may use different definition – for example, the one used by Mensa defines IQ with a mean of 100 but where 95% of the population score between 60 and 140! So a score of 140 on the Mensa test corresponds to a score of 130 on the UK *Test the Nation* test. To convert from one to another, you need to know the 'standard deviation' of the two tests. If you have taken a test with a standard deviation of 15, what would your score be on a test with a standard deviation of 20, such as the Mensa test?

If your IQ is greater than 100 (for example, 120), simply calculate: IQ = 100 + (120 − 100) × (20 ÷ 15) = 100 + 27, or 127.

If your IQ was less than 100 (say 90), calculate: IQ = 100 − (100 − 90) × (20 ÷ 15), or 87.

(b) The second possibility is that the other test you took was standardized a long time ago; the Flynn effect (see Chapter 4) means that it would now overestimate your IQ.

(c) The third possibility is that the other test was poorly constructed and/or not normed on a proper representative sample of the population. I would be particularly concerned with Internet-based tests, where no one can know the *real* ages of the participants, or whether they start guessing the answers at random if/when they get bored. Those that I have seen do not specify how they were normed, and without this information the results are meaningless. Good IQ tests are usually commercial products as they take a lot of time and money to develop, and administering the items to a random sample of the population is hugely expensive. Care is taken to keep the items secret, so that people who may be given the test when seeking employment, etc. would not have been able to find and memorize the correct answers in advance. So it is highly unlikely that an Internet-based test would be as well constructed as one used commercially, or on *Test the Nation*.

(d) Your score may have been underestimated on one occasion – for example, through anxiety, fatigue, alcohol or distraction.

I got a low IQ. Does this mean that I am a failure?
Absolutely not! Half the people in the population score below average on the test and it is possible that there may be a reason why your score was underestimated (anxiety, fatigue, distraction, alcohol...). In any case, the margin of error discussed above means that some people's scores will have been underestimated, although most will not have been. But even if your score is both low and accurate, it certainly doesn't mean there is anything wrong with you – IQ is only one aspect of your life. The test score suggests you probably don't excel at things requiring clear, logical thought – but you may well have great social skills, a talent for enthusing people, sensitivity to other people's feelings and a whole host of other desirable and useful characteristics. Speaking personally, some of the most

unpleasant people I have met probably had IQs well over 130, and its important to remember that being successful doesn't rely on your IQ alone.

This book has focused on what IQ can tell us about a person, and it is clear that it can predict performance in several situations. But I hope no one comes away with the impression that it is the only thing that matters about an individual. Personality, standards, interests and beliefs, and the ability to make relationships with others, probably matter just as much in day-to-day life.

Aren't these tests very old-fashioned? I thought psychology had moved on from this sort of stuff.
Yes – the types of tests used to assess IQ these days are not radically different from those used in the 1930s. We have discovered more primary abilities, and have a much better idea of the structure of abilities – so when devising a test we can ensure that it assesses all (or most) of the main second-order abilities. But if these tests do a good job of assessing IQ, why should one need to change the format radically? The links between IQ and everyday life shown in Chapter 7, and the associations between IQ tests and biological variables discussed in Chapter 8, show that traditional tests have considerable theoretical and practical utility. Furthermore, although some more recent theories have claimed to supplant IQ (Gardner's theory of multiple intelligences being a prime example: see Chapter 2) the evidence usually shows that these are either compatible with the existing hierarchical model of abilities (Gardner's intelligences are ability factors) or poorly supported by empirical data (i.e., just plain wrong). The structure of intelligence is not really an issue any longer, nor has it been since the 1970s. Since then researchers have indeed moved on to study what social, biological and cognitive mechanisms cause different people to perform at different levels when solving problems in IQ tests.

Surely it's not possible to describe a person's mental abilities using just one simple number, their IQ?

It all depends how much accuracy you want. You could spend several days assessing many tens of primary mental abilities, which will give you an accurate picture. The hierarchical model (discussed in Chapter 2) shows that it is possible to measure about eight second-order ability factors instead (this might take just a few hours). Or you could just plump for a single test measuring general intelligence (IQ). Given the finding that for most applications the amount of general intelligence assessed by a test predicts performance (see Chapter 7), there is probably not much to be lost by using a straightforward, quick test of general ability. Occupational psychologists who may well have to ensure that the tests they use assess the skills required in a particular job (and who get paid for devising new tests!) will devise a variety of specialized tests for each new customer. But as all ability tests measure general ability to some extent, it is quite possible that such tests actually work because of the 'active ingredient' of general ability.

Why do the items in different IQ tests look so different?

Some test-constructors take the line we took in *Test the Nation* and include a wide range of items. The advantage of doing this is that if anyone has a great strength in one area (for example, using numbers) this will be reflected in the test score, but will not dominate it – the *whole* test does not involve numbers. (It also makes for more interesting television than showing many near-identical problems.) Another approach involves identifying types of problems that are particularly good measures of general intelligence: verbal analogies of the type 'grass is to field as water is to ocean/wet/blue/ship' are particularly good measures of general ability, and so a test containing just these types of items would probably be quite effective (if tedious to take). But the bottom line is that it does not really matter too much what a test includes, as long as the items are well written, unbiased and of appropriate difficulty. As far as I am aware, every single ability test that has ever been constructed measures general ability to some extent, even though their authors may sometimes wish and/or pretend otherwise.

In some of the analyses of group differences, following 'Test the Nation', why did those who live in small towns, or support unpopular sports clubs always seem to come out top?

There is a simple statistical explanation for this. If only two or three supporters of a particular club take part in an IQ test it is not that improbable that all of them will be really clever, which will lead to a high average IQ for supporters of the club. (It could equally be quite a lot lower than average.) But if there is another club for which 10,000 people provide IQ data, the chances of all 10,000 'just happening' to be above the mean will be tiny. So if there is really little or no difference between groups, the ones with the fewest members always give the most extreme (high, and low) scores.

I scored 108. My friend scored 106. So I'm brighter – right?

Perhaps – but you can't be sure. Because there is a margin of error associated with each person's score on the test (see 'How accurate is my score', above), and if the difference between two people is small compared with it, it is hard to be certain who is the more intelligent. Your extra two points could easily have arisen because you were lucky enough to guess one item correctly, whereas your friend did not. It's not sensible to conclude that one person is smarter than another unless the difference is quite substantial – say 15 or more IQ points – and even then there will be a faint chance that the two are of equal ability.

Are men smarter than women?

Men perform rather better at items involving shapes and women perform better at items involving language.[2] In the interest of fairness most tests are anyway constructed so that both sexes score the same. So, no.

Is there a link between intelligence and which star sign you're born under?

Surprisingly, the old literature does show some relationship between month of birth and IQ.[3] Forlano and Erlich[4] found that children who were born in spring or summer tended to be slightly more intelligent than those born in autumn or winter. The differences are, however, very small – just one or two points of IQ. Curiously, there is a much larger tendency for very eminent people (those listed in the *Encyclopaedia Britannica*) to be born in February rather than midsummer. Of course, this does not mean that a person's star sign influences their IQ, or that horoscopes predestine people's lives. It is much more likely that the temperature or types of nutrition available to mothers at various months of the year may have impacted on foetal development, particularly as the studies were carried out a long time ago before central heating, shopping malls and freezers were widely available.

If I have a high IQ can I ask my boss for a pay rise?

Why not try! Point out that the research shows that the people who perform better in any job tend to be the most intelligent. But surely your boss will have already noticed that you are outperforming all your colleagues and rewarded you accordingly...

Will I live longer if I have a higher IQ?

There is clear evidence from following up members of the Scottish Mental Survey (see Chapter 4) that there is a fairly substantial relationship between childhood IQ and whether or not the person died by age 76. (War-related deaths were excluded.) The intelligent boys and girls tended to outlive the less intelligent ones. Other studies have also shown that higher levels of IQ may be associated with a lower risk of dementia in old age.

How can I make my low IQ score higher?
See Chapters 5 and 6.

Does intelligence depend on birth order?
It used to be thought that there was a (small) association between IQ and the order in which children were born in a family, with the early born being more intelligent than the later born. Recent studies which have followed up children into adulthood suggest there is no appreciable difference due to birth order, and that the small effects noted before were probably flawed in their methodology.[5]

If I keep doing IQ tests will my intelligence increase?
Your *scores* will increase to a limited extent, though the benefits are greatest in the first few hours spent doing them. It probably does not mean that your IQ will increase – you probably won't perform any better at exams or at work, for example.

Are people who go to university more intelligent?
It depends how universities select their students. As performance at academic examinations is linked to IQ, if the university uses school-leaving examination performance or an ability test (such as the Scholastic Aptitude Test) to select candidates, they are bound to be. Recent research by Margaret McRorie and myself showed that a sample of 70 Queen's University, Belfast, psychology students had a mean IQ of 111.

My mum has a high IQ. Will I?
You share half your mother's genetic make-up and, as this

affects your adult intelligence, you are more likely than not to have an above-average IQ too. But this certainly cannot be guaranteed. A lot depends on what you do outside the family environment. Also, the way you are brought up (the 'shared environment') will affect your IQ until you are about 14.

My parents are stupid. Am I stupid too?

One of the big advantages of IQ being substantially inherited is that it guarantees that the children within a family will vary in their IQs. If we consider just the genes that vary from person to person, each child only shares about half of them with their brothers and sisters. Some will have struck lucky and received all the genes that predispose them towards developing a high IQ; others will not. Most will receive about half; some will receive less. There is also a tendency for children's IQs to be closer to the average than their parents'. So, if parents are not that intelligent there will be substantial variation between the IQs of the children, and the average IQ of the children will probably be slightly higher than the parents' IQs. So the short answer is 'Quite probably not'. It would be a much more depressing scenario if IQ was entirely shaped by the family environment. In that case children born to low-income, socially deprived parents would not have a chance of developing a high IQ.

Will I become smarter if I talk or associate with smarter people?

It is difficult to know the answer to this one, as it is necessary to ask whether associating with smarter people makes you intelligent, or whether because you are intelligent you tend to mix with smarter people. It would be difficult to tease this relationship out unless one could measure the IQs of children before and after they were randomly assigned to associating with either low- or high-ability friends. I cannot see how this experiment could be carried out in practice, even if it were ethical to do so.

Will I become smarter if I read lots of books?

See the answer to the previous question. Are you intelligent because you read? Or do you choose to read because you are intelligent? There will be some people with language problems (dyslexia) who otherwise have high IQs, but for most children IQ seems to have a fairly substantial correlation with reading skills.[6]

I read a tabloid newspaper – am I more or less intelligent than someone who reads a broadsheet?

The vocabulary used in tabloid newspapers is less rarefied than that used in broadsheets. Thus it is likely that someone who chooses to read a broadsheet is able to understand the more advanced vocabulary and sentence structure, and also take an interest in important – but more abstract – issues, such as global warming or health-service reform. So, although I cannot find any data on the subject, I strongly suspect that most readers of broadsheets will be of higher than average IQ, although some high-IQ individuals will undoubtedly read tabloids (for example, out of habit, or because other people in the family insist on buying them).

Eating fish, especially tuna, makes you smarter. Is this true?

Attempts have been made to boost IQ by giving children vitamin supplements, and these initially seemed to be surprisingly effective, although it now appears that the effects are only found in children (quite a lot of them) who do not eat particularly nutritious diets. One study has looked at the effect of giving young babies a fish-oil dietary supplement, and it did not seem to boost their abilities – but the children were tested at a very young age so the results may not be reliable. However, most of the literature examines the effects on IQ of toxins in fish. Pregnant mothers should clearly avoid polluted fish!

My IQ is above average yet I'm not rich. Why not?
Your IQ is only one part of your character. Many high-IQ people will decide, for example, that they do not want to be part of the rat race and become organic farmers in the depths of the country. Or you may not have obtained the educational qualifications that are necessary to enter a profession. Or you may have chosen to embark on a career that is fulfilling but badly paid – lecturing at university or nursing being obvious examples.

If I have an above-average IQ will I marry someone similar?
This is quite likely. Research has shown that a high IQ is a quality that we value when looking for a mate.[7] It has also been found that partners' IQs are far more similar than would be expected by chance. The correlation is in the order of 0.4[8] which is higher than that for any personality trait of which I am aware. It really does seem as if we choose a partner with a broadly similar level of intelligence to our own.

Postscript

This book has tried to give a balanced overview of some of the important and interesting issues in intelligence research, and I hope readers now share some of my enthusiasm for the topic. If you want to find out more, there are several good books available, including those by Nicholas Mackintosh at Cambridge[1], Ian Deary at Edinburgh[2] and Nathan Brody from New Hampshire.[3] There are many others too, but these three give a good, balanced account of the area and are written by active researchers. My introductory text on intelligence[4] may also be of interest. The other option is, of course, to study the subject further. At this stage you will have an idea of your own IQ, and so may well contemplate studying psychology in evening classes or at a university. If you decide to do so you should remember that IQ, personality, etc. is only a small part of the psychology syllabus, and universities vary enormously in the amount of time they devote to it.

I first encountered the topic of intelligence in some of Paul Kline's inspirational lectures at Exeter in the 1970s. Thirty years on it still amazes me that scores obtained from a simple test lasting just an hour or two can predict so much about a person's behaviour – not just their educational level or the sort of job they end up doing, but how well they get on within their chosen career, the length of their life, the number of physical and psychiatric problems they encounter, the characteristics of the person they marry, their likelihood of dying in an accident, the chances of developing Alzheimer's dizease and a whole host of other things. None of these relationships are anywhere near perfect, of course. But they are all way beyond what you would expect by chance. IQ does seem to be important.

When one tries to explore what makes people develop their particular level of IQ, the picture becomes even more intriguing. I would never have expected that the sorts of variation between families in western society (money, attitudes to education, availability of books, etc.) have no impact whatsoever on the IQ of adults. Who would have thought that something as simple as the speed with which a person can recognize a simple shape (as in inspection time) would predict IQ? And what is causing the standard of performance at IQ tests to rise inexorably from year to year? These are interesting times for research in intelligence and IQ.

Notes

Chapter 1:
Intelligence, mental
abilities and tests

1. E.G. Boring, 'Intelligence as the tests test it', *The New Republic* (June 1923), pp. 35–7.

Chapter 2:
The discovery of
General Intelligence

1. C.A. Spearman, 'General Intelligence objectively determined and measured', *American Journal of Psychology* **15** (1904), pp. 201–93.
2. L.L. Thurstone, *Primary Mental Abilities* (University of Chicago Press, 1938).
3. J.B. Carroll, *Human Cognitive Abilities: A survey of factor-analytic studies* (Cambridge University Press, 1993).
4. C. Cooper, *Intelligence and Abilities* (Routledge, London, 1999), pp. 36–37
5. H. Gardner, *Frames of Mind*, 2nd edn (HarperCollins, London, 1993).
6. D. Goleman, *Emotional Intelligence* (Bantam Books, New York, 1995).

Chapter 3:
Interpreting test scores

1. L.J. Kamin, *The Science and Politics of IQ* (Penguin, Harmondsworth, 1974).

Chapter 4:
Changing abilities

1. I.J. Deary, L.J. Whalley, H. Lemmon, J.R. Crawford and J.M. Starr, 'Stability of individual differences in mental ability from childhood to old age: follow-up of the 1932 Scottish Mental Survey', *Intelligence* **28** (2000), pp. 49–55.
2. S.R. Pinneau, *Changes in Intelligence Quotient: Infancy to Maturity* (Houghton-Mifflin, New York, 1961).
3. J.R. Flynn, 'Searching for justice: the discovery of IQ gains over time', *American Psychologist* **54** (1999), pp 5–20.
4. R.W. Howard, 'Searching the real world for signs of rising population intelligence', *Personality and Individual Differences* **30** (2001), pp. 1039–58.
5. M. Anderson, *Intelligence and Development* (Blackwell, Oxford, 1992).
6. N. Brody, *Intelligence* (Academic Press, San Diego CA, 1992).

Chapter 5:
Boosting IQ

1. I.J. Deary, L.J. Whalley, H. Lemmon, J.R. Crawford and J.M. Starr, 'Stability of individual differences in mental ability from childhood to old age: follow-up of the 1932 Scottish Mental Survey', *Intelligence* **28** (2000), pp. 49–55.
2. H.L. Garber and M.J. Begab, *The Milwaukee Project: Preventing mental retardation in children at risk* (American Association on Mental Retardation, Washington DC, 1988).
3. C.T. Ramey and F.A. Campbell, 'The Carolina Abecederian Project', in J.G. Gallagher and C.T. Ramey (eds), *The Malleability of Children* (Paul H. Brookes, Baltimore MD, 1987), pp. 127–39.
4. N. Brody, *Intelligence* (Academic

Press, San Diego CA, 1992).

5. M. Egan and B. Bunting, 'The effects of coaching on 11+ scores', *British Journal of Educational Psychology* **61** (1991), pp. 85–91.

6. H.J. Eysenck, *Know Your Own IQ* (Penguin, Harmondsworth, 1962).

Chapter 7:
IQ and everyday life

1. See, for example, S.J. Gould, *The Mismeasure of Man* (Norton, New York, 1996).

2. See, for example, M.J.A. Howe, *IQ in Question* (Sage, London, 1997).

3. R.E. Snow and E. Yallow, 'Education and intelligence', in R.J. Sternberg (ed.), *Handbook of Human Intelligence* (Cambridge University Press, 1982), pp. 493–585.

4. A.R. Jensen, *The g Factor* (Praeger, Westport CT, 1998).

5. C.A. Spearman, 'General Intelligence objectively determined and measured', *American Journal of Psychology*, **15** (1904), pp. 201–93.

6. W.F. Horn and T. Packard, 'Early identification of learning problems', *Journal of Educational Psychology* **77** (1985), pp. 597–607.

7. N. Brody, *Intelligence* (Academic Press, San Diego CA, 1992).

8. A.D. DeGroot, 'War and the intelligence of youth', *Journal of Abnormal and Social Psychology* **46** (1951), pp. 596–97.

9. S. Cahan and N. Cohen, 'Age versus schooling effects on intelligence development', *Child Development* **60** (1989), pp. 1239–49.

10. N.F. Dixon, *On the Psychology of Military Incompetence* (Basic Books, New York, 1976).

11. R.L. Thorndike, 'The central role of general ability in prediction', *Multivariate Behavioral Research* **20** (1985), pp. 241–54.

12. A.R. Jensen, *The g Factor* (Praeger, Westport CT, 1998).

13. Ibid, p. 284.

14. T.W. Harrell and M.S. Harrell, 'Army general classification test scores for civilian occupations', *Educational and Psychological Measurement* **5** (1945), pp. 229–39.

15. J.E. Hunter and R.F. Hunter, 'Validity and utility of alternative predictors of job performance', *Psychological Bulletin* **96** (1984), pp. 72–98.

16. P.L. Kanfer, Y.M. Ackerman and M. Goff, 'Personality and intelligence in industrial and organizational psychology', in D.H. Saklofske and M. Zeidner (eds), *International Handbook of Personality and Intelligence* (Plenum, New York, 1995), p. 597.

17. B.J. O'Toole and L. Stankov, 'Ultimate validity of psychological tests', *Personality and Individual Differences* **13** (1992), pp. 699–716.

18. D. Lubinski and L.G. Humphreys, 'Some bodily and medical correlates of mathematical giftedness and commensurate levels of socioeconomic status', *Intelligence* **16** (1992), pp. 99–115.

19. B. Schmand, J.H. Smit, M.I. Geerlings and J. Lindeboom, 'The effects of intelligence and education on the development of dementia. A test of the brain reserve hypothesis', *Psychological Medicine* **27** (1997), 1337–44.

20. N.P. Walker, P.M. McConville, D. Hunter, I.J. Deary and L.J. Whalley, 'Childhood mental ability and lifetime psychiatric contact – a 66-

year follow-up study of the 1932 Scottish Mental Ability Survey', *Intelligence* **30** (2002), pp 233–45.

21. R.J. Herrnstein and R. Murray, *The Bell Curve* (Free Press, New York, 1994).

22. R.A. Gordon, 'SES versus IQ in the race-IQ-delinquency model', *International Journal of Sociology and Social Policy* **7** (1987), pp. 30–96.

23. C.M. Steele and J. Aronson, 'Stereotype threat and the intellectual test performance of African Americans', *Journal of Personality and Social Psychology* **69** (1995), pp. 797–811.

24. A.R. Jensen, *Bias in Mental Testing* (Free Press, New York, 1980).

25. B. Tizard, 'IQ and race', *Nature* **247** (1974), p. 316.

26. K. Eyferth, 'Leistungen verschiedener Gruppen von Besatzungskindern in Hamburg', *Archiv fur die gesamte Psychologie* **113** (1961), pp. 222–41. Cited in N. Brody, op cit.

27. R.A. Weinberg, S. Scarr and I.D. Waldman, 'The Minnesota Transracial Adoption Study', *Intelligence* **16** (1992), pp. 117–35.

Chapter 8:
Current issues

1. R.C. Tryon, 'Genetic differences in maze-learning ability in rats', *Yearbook of the National Society of Student Education* **39** (1940), pp. 111–19.

2. N. Segal, 'Same-age unrelated siblings: a unique test of within-family environmental influences on IQ similarity', *Journal of Educational Psychology* **89** (1997), pp. 381–90.

3. R. Plomin, 'The nature and nurture of human cognitive abilities', in R.J. Sternberg (ed.), *Advances in the Psychology of Human Intelligence* (Erlbaum, Hillsdale NJ, 1988).

4. L.J. Kamin, *The Science and Politics of IQ* (Penguin, Harmondsworth, 1974).

5. R. Plomin and S.A. Petrill, 'Genetics and intelligence: what's new?', *Intelligence* **24** (1997), pp. 53–77.

6. E.B. Hunt, 'The mechanics of verbal ability', *Psychological Review* **85** (1978), pp. 109–30.

7. N.J. Mackintosh, *IQ and Human Intelligence* (Oxford University Press, 1998).

8. A.R. Jensen and S.N. Sinha, 'Physical correlates of human intelligence', in P.A. Vernon (ed.), *Biological Approaches to the Study of Human Intelligence* (Ablex, New York, 1993), pp. 139–242. Outlines the main gender differences in some detail.

9. A.R. Jensen, *The g Factor* (Praeger, Westport CT, 1998).

10. See, for example, J.K. Grudnik and J.H. Kranzler, 'Meta-analysis of the relationship between intelligence and inspection time', *Intelligence* **29** (2001), pp. 523–35.

11. A. Anokhin and F. Vogel, 'EEG alpha-frequency and intelligence in normal adults', *Intelligence* **23** (1996), pp.1–14.

12. T.E. Reed and A.R. Jensen, 'Conduction velocity in a brain nerve pathway correlates with intelligence level', *Intelligence* **16** (1992), pp. 259–72.

13. R.J. Haier, 'Cerebral glucose metabolism and intelligence', in P.A. Vernon (ed.), *Biological Approaches to the Study of Human Intelligence* (Ablex, New York, 1992), pp. 317–332.

Chapter 9:
Some frequently asked questions about intelligence

1. J.C. Wickett, P.A. Vernon and D.H. Lee, 'Relationships between the factors of intelligence and brain volume', *Personality and Individual Differences* **29** (2000), pp. 1095–1122.
2. D.F. Halpern, *Sex Differences in Cognitive Abilities*, 2nd edn (Erlbaum, Hillsdale NJ, 1992).
3. H.J. Eysenck and D.K.B. Nias, *Astrology: Science or superstition?* (St Martin's Press, New York, 1982).
4. Cited by Eysenck and Nias ibid.
5. J. L. Rodgers, 'What causes birth order-intelligence patterns? The admixture hypothesis, revived', *American Psychologist* **56** (2001), pp. 505–10.
6. J.A. Naglieri, 'An examination of the relationship between intelligence and reading achievement using the MAT-SF and MAST', *Journal of Psychoeducational Assessment* **14** (1996), pp. 65–9.
7. S. Sprecher and P.C. Regan, 'Liking some things (in some people) more than others' *Journal of Social and Personal Relationships* **19** (2002), pp. 463–81.
8. A.R. Jensen, *The g Factor* (Praeger, Westport CT, 1998).

Postscript

1. N.J. Mackintosh, *IQ and Human Intelligence* (Oxford University Press, 1998).
2. I.J. Deary, *Looking Down on Human Intelligence* (Oxford University Press, 2000).
3. N. Brody, *Intelligence* (Academic Press, San Diego CA, 1992).
4. C. Cooper, *Intelligence and Abilities* (Routledge, London, 1999).

Appendix A

The IQ test in Appendix B is the one that was administered on *Test the Nation*, broadcast on BBC television during May 2002. It is included in this book to show what the items in a typical IQ test involve. Whilst you may wish to sit it and estimate your IQ you should remember the following:

- If you have flicked through the test and seen the items or answers, or if you have already taken it on the Internet or television, you will probably overestimate your IQ.
- The test was designed and standardized by presenting items on a large screen and the time given to solve each item was accurately controlled. We simply do not know the extent to which scores on the printed version of the test will be similar to those on the original version. The printed test could well systematically under- or overestimate IQ.
- A number of factors (for example, nervousness, alcohol, familiarity with the English language, previous experience of taking the test or looking at the items, distractions, the accuracy of the timing of the items) may influence whether or not the scores are accurate. If you do decide to take the test 'for real' you need to ensure that you are alert, completely sober, that you have not seen any of the test items before – even briefly – and that a friend times each item for you.

The basic message is that because we do not know whether the printed version of the test is precisely as difficult as the televised version, have no control over how it is administered and cannot tell whether a person has seen the items before, it is impossible to know how accurate the scores on the test will be. So, if your score is high you should not assume that you are a genius – and if it is low you should not be in the least concerned!

Administering the IQ test

The test consists of 70 items divided into 13 sections. Each section begins with a practice item – an example to show you what to do – followed by between four and six individually timed test items. You should take as long as you need to look at the practice items for each section, but will have to ask a friend to help you with timing the test ones. He or she should call out 'next' after the times shown in Table 1 have elapsed and you should immediately move on to the next item, guessing an answer at random if you have not managed to solve the problem. If you finish an item before time is called, please fight the temptation to look ahead at future items or go back and spend more time on previous ones! Instructions for scoring and interpreting the results are given in Appendix C. If you want your test score to be as accurate as possible you should not look at this until after you have taken the test.

Item number	Description	Number of items	Time per item
1–5	Vocabulary	5	10 seconds
6–10	Proverbs	5	25 seconds
11–15	Memory for addresses	5	30 seconds to memorize; 15 seconds to recall
16–21	Nonverbal series completion	6	15 seconds
22–26	Number series	5	20 seconds
27–31	Shape series	5	15 seconds
32–37	Verbal analogies	6	20 seconds
38–43	Mental arithmetic	6	15 seconds
44–48	Mathematical puzzles	5	30 seconds
49–53	Using objects	5	20 seconds
54–59	Mental rotation	6	20 seconds
60–65	Paper folding	6	20 seconds
66–70	Hidden shapes	5	20 seconds

Table 1: Timings for the 70-item IQ test in Appendix B.

the
national
IQ test

Appendix B - The National IQ Test

You should begin by writing down the numbers 1–70 on a sheet of paper, leaving a little space next to each number for you to write down your answer. For each problem, choose one of the four alternatives and write A, B, C or D next to the question number.

You should NOT write down the answers for the practice items, which are there to show you how to tackle the problems in that section.

You will need to use a stopwatch (or a friend's help) to ensure that you keep to the time limits for each question.

Part 1 – Vocabulary (10 seconds each)

Example
Which word means the same as 'replace':

A Adjust
B Move
C Reprieve
D *Substitute*

1. Which word means the same as 'engine':

A Car
B Power
C Petrol
D Motor

2. Which word means the same as 'frail':

A Feeble
B Ancient
C Sick
D Unhappy

3. Which word means the same as 'hardly':

A Toughly
B Slowly
C Reluctantly
D Scarcely

4. Which word means the same as 'furtive'?

A Stealthy
B Silent
C Guilty
D Angry

5. Which of the following means the same as 'feint'?

A Fall over
B Anger
C Make a deceptive movement
D Map

Part 2 – Proverbs (25 seconds each)

Example
Which saying means 'act quickly':

A Fools rush in where angels fear to tread.
B In for a penny, in for a pound.
C *He who hesitates is lost.*
D Remember the boy who cried wolf.

6. Which saying means 'we learn from experience'?

A Once bitten, twice shy.
B A chain is no stronger than its weakest link.
C While the cat's away the mice will play.
D Birds of a feather flock together.

7. Which saying means 'to go from a bad to a worse situation'?

A Caught between the devil and the deep blue sea.
B Out of the frying pan, into the fire.
C Here today, gone tomorrow.
D A miss is as good as a mile.

8. Which saying means 'people vary':

A When in Rome do as the Romans do.
B A wink is a good as a nod.
C People who live in glass houses shouldn't throw stones.
D One man's meat is another man's poison.

9. Which saying means 'calamities often occur together'?

   A   Cut your coat according to the cloth.
   B   It never rains but it pours.
   C   The darkest hour is before the dawn.
   D   If you lie down with dogs, you'll get up with fleas.

10. Which saying means 'it is easy to be jealous'?

   A   He has enough who is content.
   B   Possession is nine-tenths of the law.
   C   The grass is always greener on the other side of the fence.
   D   Sauce for the goose is sauce for the gander.

Part 3 – Memory for information (30 + 15 seconds)

You have 30 seconds to memorize an address or other information. You will then have 15 seconds to answer a question on it.

Example

Janette Brown
48 Hounslow Road
Twickenham
ITW1 4YT

What was the correct name?

- **A**   Janet Brown
- **B**   Jannette Browne
- **C**   Janette Brown
- **D**   Janet Browne

11. Memorize these details:

Dr Steven Frank
47 Woodside Grove
St Austell
PL25 3UX

What is the postcode?

- **A**   PL23 5UX
- **B**   PL25 3UX
- **C**   PL55 3UY
- **D**   PL35 5UX

12. Memorize these details:

Jignesh Patel
Supreme Carpets
Binsberg Industrial Estate
Hagley Road West
Birmingham
B32 9ZQ

Which one of the following is INCORRECT?

A Binsberg Industrial Estate
B B32 9ZQ
C Mrs B G Davis
D Hagley Road West

13. Memorize these details:

Clifford Morgan
The South Wales Angler
18 Westlake Avenue
Cardiff
CF1 3BQ

What is the house number and street?

A 80 Westlake Avenue
B 80 West Drake Avenue
C 18 West Lake Avenue
D 18 Westlake Avenue

14. Memorize these details:

Department 8F–KC/931
The Emetic Elevator Corporation
Unit 86
Lower Lochboisdale Crescent
Galashiels
TD1 8FQ

Which part is INCORRECT?

A Lower Lochboisdale Crescent
B 8F–KC/3931
C Unit 86
D TDF1 8FQ

15. Memorize this newsagent's list:

Julie Bull – *Radio Times, Sun, Mirror*

Helen Baxter – *Hello!, Guardian, Private Eye*

Paula Ferris – *Telegraph, Mac User, Good Housekeeping*

Susan Murray – *Farmer's Weekly, Times, Woman's Own*

What papers and magazines did Helen Baxter take?

A *Hello!, Mirror, Good Housekeeping*
B *Sun, Mirror, Good Housekeeping*
C *Hello!, Guardian, Private Eye*
D *Radio Times, Sun, Mirror*

Part 4 - Nonverbal series completion (15 seconds each)

Example

The 3 figures on the top line change according to a sequence. Choose the 1 figure from the bottom line that completes the sequence.

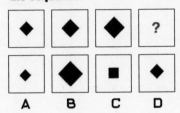

16. Complete the series:

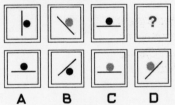

17. Complete the series:

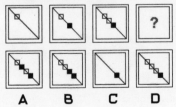

18. Complete the series:

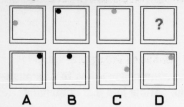

    A   B   C   D

19. Complete the series:

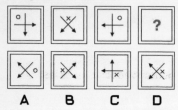

    A   B   C   D

20. Complete the series:

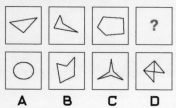

    A   B   C   D

21. Complete the series:

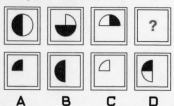

    A   B   C   D

Part 5 - Number series (20 seconds each)

Example

Choose the next number that continues the series:

2 4 7 11 ?

A 13
B 19
C **16**
D 17

22. Choose the next number that continues the series:

999 333 111 37 ?

A 13
B 12
C 12.33
D 13.33

23. Choose the next number that continues the series:

1 2 3 5 8 13 ?

A 25
B 26
C 23
D 21

24. Choose the next number that continues the series:

11 10 13 8 15 6 ?

A 17
B 11
C 13
D 19

25. Choose the next number that continues the series:

13 21 34 55 89 ?

A 113
B 105
C 144
D 125

26. Choose the next number that continues the series:

32 16 24 20 ?

A 22
B 26
C 40
D 18

Part 6 - Shape series (15 seconds each)

Example

Which shape completes the series?

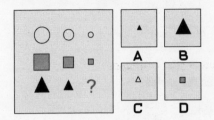

27. Which shape completes the series?

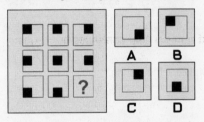

28. Which shape completes the series?

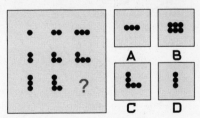

29. Which shape completes the series?

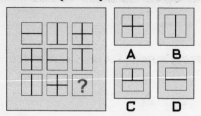

30. Which shape completes the series?

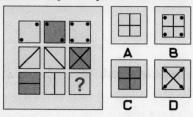

31. Which shape completes the series?

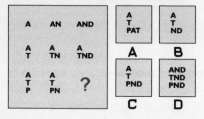

Part 7 - Verbal analogies (20 seconds each)

Example

Which word has the same relation to the third word as the second has to the first?

Food is to hunger as water is to

A *Thirst*
B Drink
C Wet
D Liquid

32. **Which word has the same relation to the third word as the second has to the first?**

    Tadpole is to frog as caterpillar is to

    A Garden
    B Air
    C Pond
    D Butterfly

33. **Which word has the same relation to the third word as the second has to the first?**

    Long is to short as fat is to

    A Small
    B Thin
    C Narrow
    D Broad

34. Which word has the same relation to the third word as the second has to the first?

Grape is to wine as flour is to

A Wheat
B Dough
C Baker
D Oven

35. Which word has the same relation to the third word as the second has to the first?

Circle is to square as ball is to

A Rectangle
B Cube
C Tennis
D Bat

36. Which word has the same relation to the third word as the second has to the first?

Microscope is to microbe as amplifier is to

A Loudspeaker
B Whisper
C Listen
D Microphone

37. Which word has the same relation to the third word as the second has to the first?

Picasso is to Constable as bus is to

A Train
B Brush
C Travel
D Stagecoach

Part 7 – Mental arithmetic (15 seconds each)

Example

Add up the following numbers and choose the right answer

$1 + 2 + 3 + 4 + 5 + 6 + 7 = ?$

A *28*
B 26
C 29
D 30

38. Add up the following numbers and choose the right answer

$2 + 7 + 3 + 8 + 5 + 7 + 8 = ?$

   A 39
   B 40
   C 42
   D 45

39. If X=3 and Y=7
X + (X x Y) = ?

   A 30
   B 13
   C 24
   D 63

40. $\dfrac{59}{X} = 118$ What is X?

   A 0.5
   B 2
   C 20
   D 177

41. What is the average of these numbers?

1408 1412 1414

A 1408
B 1409
C 1410
D 5636

42. $\dfrac{9}{139 + 43}$

Expressed as a percentage is approximately

A 2%
B 5%
C 9%
D 18%

43. 37 x 271 is approximately

A 1000
B 6000
C 8000
D 10000

Part 8 - Mathematical puzzles (30 seconds each)

Example

A car uses 12 litres of petrol to travel 100 miles. How many litres would be used for a 350-mile journey?

A *42*
B 125
C 37
D 50

44. **A supply of food will keep 9 people for 12 days. How long would it keep 3 people?**

    A 48 days
    B 24 days
    C 27 days
    D 36 days

45. **A car travels 8 miles in 10 minutes. What is the distance it travels in 1 hour?**

    A 48 miles
    B 80 miles
    C 60 miles
    D 75 miles

46. **Interest on savings is taxed at a rate of 20%. A bank statement shows that you have £10 interest after tax. How much interest did you have before the tax was deducted?**

    A £8
    B £12
    C £12.50
    D £11

47. The price of car parking has increased from 25p to 35p per 15-minute period. What is the increase as a percentage?

    A 60%

    B 20%

    C 71%

    D 40%

48. A 50m-long cable is divided so that 1 piece is 2/3 of the length of the other piece. How long is the shorter piece?

    A 24m

    B 20m

    C 16m

    D 18m

Part 9 - Using objects (20 seconds)

Example

Which ladder is safely positioned against the wall?

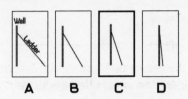

49. **Which vase is most likely to fall over?**

50. **Where should the 50kg weight be hung in order to balance the scales?**

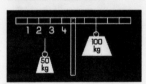

A at 1
B at 2
C at 3
D at 4

51. Which wheelbarrow can be lifted with the LEAST effort?

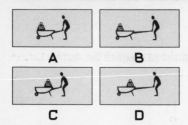

52. Out of which reservoir will the water stream with the highest pressure?

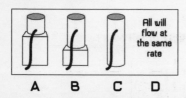

53. Some provisions were thrown out of an aeroplane at Point X. Where do they land?

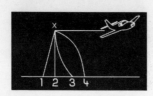

A At 1
B At 2
C At 3
D At 4

Part 10 - Mental rotation (20 seconds each)

Example

Out of the four shapes, find the one which cannot be turned round to lie on top of the others.

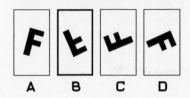

A   B   C   D

54. Which is the odd one out?

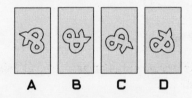

A   B   C   D

55. Which is the odd one out?

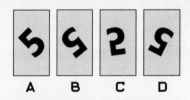

A   B   C   D

56. Which is the odd one out?

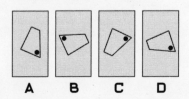

A   B   C   D

57. Which is the odd one out?

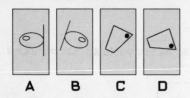

A   B   C   D

58. Which is the odd one out?

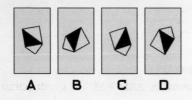

A   B   C   D

59. Which is the odd one out?

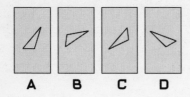

A   B   C   D

Part 11 – Paper folding (20 seconds)

Example

Which solid shape could be made by folding the shape on the left?

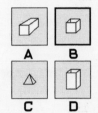

60. Which solid shape could be made from the paper pattern?

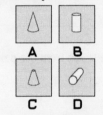

61. Which solid shape could be made from the paper pattern?

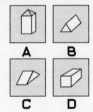

62. **Which paper pattern could be used to make the solid shape?**

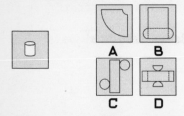

63. **Which solid shape could be made from the paper pattern?**

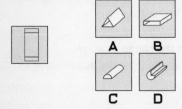

64. **Which solid shape could be made from the paper pattern?**

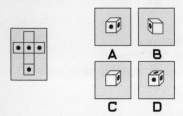

65. **Which paper pattern could be used to make the solid shape?**

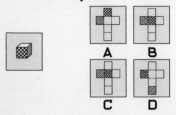

Part 12 – Hidden shapes (20 seconds each)

Example

Which figure below contains the shape shown?

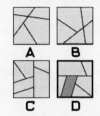

66. Which figure below contains the shape shown?

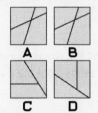

67. Which figure below contains the shape shown?

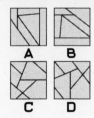

68. Which figure below contains the shape shown?

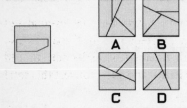

69. Which figure below contains the shape shown?

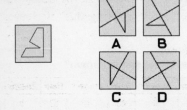

70. Which figure below contains the shape shown?

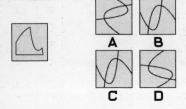

Appendix C

The items in the test in Appendix B have been factor-analysed and they form a single factor. The reliability of the test is also very satisfactory (**0.85**). This means it is legitimate to add together the scores on all the items, and then convert this total into an IQ.

The correct answers to the items are shown in Table 2. Simply give yourself 1 point for each of the 70 test items that you have answered correctly; you should *not* include your answers to the practice items when working out this score. Items which you have not attempted, or which you have answered incorrectly, get 0 points.

Item	Answer	Item	Answer	Item	Answer	Item	Answer	Item	Answer
1	d	15	c	29	d	43	d	57	b
2	a	16	d	30	a	44	d	58	c
3	d	17	b	31	c	45	a	59	a
4	a	18	a	32	d	46	c	60	c
5	c	19	d	33	b	47	d	61	b
6	a	20	c	34	b	48	b	62	c
7	b	21	a	35	b	49	b	63	d
8	d	22	c	36	b	50	a	64	a
9	b	23	d	37	d	51	b	65	b
10	c	24	a	38	b	52	d	66	c
11	b	25	c	39	c	53	d	67	b
12	d	26	a	40	a	54	c	68	d
13	d	27	a	41	b	55	c	69	c
14	b	28	c	42	b	56	a	70	a

Table 2: Answers for the 70-item IQ test shown in Appendix B.

Your total score shows how many of the 70 items you answered correctly – it is *not* your IQ. To estimate your IQ it is necessary to determine what proportion of people in the population obtained a score as high as yours. To do so, simply run your finger down the first column (headed 'Score/70') in Table 3 until you come to your score. Then look across that row until you find the column that shows your age group. Your IQ is the number where the row showing your score meets the column showing your age group. So, for example, a 32-year-old person who scored 49 out of 70 would have an IQ of 104. To determine what a particular IQ score means, see Chapter 3.

Score/70	Age group				
	16–19	20–34	35–54	55–69	70+
15	70	70	70	72	77
16	70	70	70	77	82
17	70	70	70	78	83
18	70	70	71	79	84
19	70	70	72	80	85
20	70	70	73	81	86
21	70	70	74	82	87
22	70	70	75	83	88
23	72	70	77	85	90
24	73	71	78	86	91
25	74	72	79	87	92
26	75	73	80	88	93
27	76	74	81	89	94
28	76	74	81	89	94
29	77	75	82	90	95
30	79	77	84	92	97
31	80	78	85	93	98
32	81	79	86	94	99
33	82	80	87	95	100
34	84	82	89	97	102
35	85	83	90	98	103
36	87	85	92	100	105
37	88	86	93	101	106
38	89	87	94	102	107
39	90	88	95	103	108

Score/70	Age group				
	16–19	20–34	35–54	55–69	70+
40	92	90	97	105	110
41	93	91	98	106	111
42	95	93	100	108	113
43	97	95	102	110	115
44	98	96	103	111	116
45	100	98	105	113	118
46	101	99	106	114	119
47	103	101	108	116	121
48	104	102	109	117	122
49	106	104	111	119	124
50	108	106	113	121	126
51	110	108	115	123	128
52	112	110	117	125	130
53	114	112	119	127	132
54	116	114	121	129	134
55	118	116	123	131	136
56	119	117	124	132	137
57	121	119	126	134	139
58	123	121	128	136	141
59	126	124	131	139	144
60	128	126	133	141	146
61	130	128	135	143	148
62	131	129	136	144	149
63	131	129	136	144	149
64	131	129	136	144	149
65	132	130	137	145	150
66	135	133	140	148	153
67	136	134	141	149	154
68	138	136	143	151	156
69	138	136	143	151	156
70	138	136	143	151	156

Table 3: Converting scores on the 70-item test to IQs.

For your score to be at all meaningful it is necessary to make the following assumptions:

- You have taken the test under ideal conditions (no distractions, etc.).
- The 200 people in the random sample of the population who took the test when it was being developed were indeed representative of the UK population.
- The difficulty of the items is the same in the printed version of the test as it was in the televised version.
- You are from the United Kingdom.
- English is your first language.

Even if you have taken the test under ideal conditions, the score you obtain will not be completely accurate – just as when a ruler is used to measure the length of an object there is always some measurement error associated with the reading. So how accurate is your IQ score likely to be? It is possible to do some statistical analyses to find out. Table 4 shows the 'margins of error' associated with each possible IQ score. It is highly likely that your 'true' IQ is somewhere between the lower and upper values shown in the table. There is less than a 1 in 20 chance that your true IQ will be outside this range. So, for example, if you obtained an IQ score of 111 from the test there is only a 5% chance that your true IQ will be below 98 or above 121.

Once again, do not panic if your IQ is lower than you would hope or expect. Whilst IQ can predict how people *generally* behave there will always be some exceptions, and you may be one of them. As discussed in Chapter 9, a person's IQ has nothing at all to do with their personality, their pleasantness or many other important characteristics. It is also possible that your score will have been underestimated because you were tired, anxious or distracted while you took the test – all the data in Table 3 and Table 4 assume that none of these factors applied. However, if you took the test under ideal conditions, and the assumptions mentioned above apply to you, your score should give some insight into how your thinking skills compare with those of other people.

IQ	Lower value	Upper value	IQ	Lower value	Upper value	IQ	Lower value	Upper value
70	63	86	97	86	109	124	109	132
71	64	87	98	87	110	125	110	133
72	65	88	99	88	111	126	110	134
73	65	89	100	88	112	127	111	135
74	66	90	101	89	112	128	112	135
75	67	90	102	90	113	129	113	136
76	68	91	103	91	114	130	114	137
77	69	92	104	92	115	131	115	138
78	70	93	105	93	116	132	116	139
79	71	94	106	93	117	133	116	140
80	71	95	107	94	118	134	117	141
81	72	95	108	95	118	135	118	141
82	73	96	109	96	119	136	119	142
83	74	97	110	97	120	137	120	143
84	75	98	111	98	121	138	121	144
85	76	99	112	99	122	139	122	145
86	76	100	113	99	123	140	122	146
87	77	101	114	100	124	141	123	146
88	78	101	115	101	124	142	124	147
89	79	102	116	102	125	143	125	148
90	80	103	117	103	126	144	126	149
91	81	104	118	104	127	145	127	150
92	82	105	119	105	128	146	127	151
93	82	106	120	105	129	147	128	152
94	83	107	121	106	129	148	129	152
95	84	107	122	107	130	149	130	153
96	85	108	123	108	131	150	131	154

Table 4: Likely margin of error for each IQ score ('95% confidence intervals').

Index